MASTERING FAMILY, LIBRARY & CHURCH RECORDS

Volume VII of *Quillen's Essentials of Genealogy*

www.essentialgenealogy.com

PRAISE FOR DAN'S BOOKS

"*Mastering Online Genealogy* written by W. Daniel Quillen is a great little book packed full of helpful tips in doing online family research ... This informative book has some great tips for beginners, as well as those who have been doing research for a while ... I look forward to reading all of the books in this genealogical series." – *Tina Sansone, Bella Online book review*

"Your book *Secrets of Tracing your Ancestors* has been extremely helpful to me in a renewal of my genealogy interests." – *Nancy Dailey*

"I would like to thank you for writing a very informative book. There was a lot of information that I did not know about..." – *Donna Perryman Moon*

"I purchased your book and have found it most helpful." – *Glenda Laney*

"Thanks for your help and for writing your excellent book!" – *Laura Johnson*

"... It is not only informative but entertaining. Incorporating your own experiences in brought the book to life. Again, thank you for helping me to understand the many aspects of genealogy and for supplying a roadmap to finding more information about our ancestors." – *Dana L. Hager*

"Of all the books I have looked at yours is the best...and you write with your heart and soul. Thanks for writing such a great book." – *Karen Dredge*

"I got this book out of the library, but before I was half-way through it, I decided I had to have my own copy. Lots of helpful suggestions! I'd recommend it for all new and experienced family historians." – *Margaret Combs*

"I am embarking on the family history journey and have found your book to be very helpful ... thanks for putting together a helpful, easy to follow guide." – *Suzanne Adams*

"I'm absolutely delighted that I discovered your book "Secrets of Tracing Your Ancestors." I've only been at this for a month (to keep sane during knee surgery recuperation) and now I'm hooked." – *Cecily Bishop*

About the Author

For the past twenty-plus years, W. Daniel Quillen has been a professional writer specializing in travel, genealogy and technical subjects. He has taught beginning genealogy courses to university students and working adults, and is a frequent lecturer in beginning and intermediate genealogy classes in Colorado. He has compiled his years of genealogical training and research into *Quillen's Essentials of Genealogy* series. He lives in Centennial, Colorado with his wife, and visits children and grandchildren in other states as often as possible (six children, four grandchildren, six states!). If you would like to contact him about anything in this book, his e-mail address is: wdanielquillen@gmail.com.

MASTERING FAMILY, LIBRARY & CHURCH RECORDS

Volume VII of *Quillen's Essentials of Genealogy*

www.essentialgenealogy.com

W. Daniel Quillen

Author of *Secrets of Tracing Your Ancestors*; *The Troubleshooter's Guide to Do-It-Yourself Genealogy*; and *Quillen's Essentials of Genealogy* books, a new series of genealogy primers

Cold Spring Press

COLD SPRING PRESS

P.O. Box 284
Cold Spring Harbor, NY 11724
E-mail: jopenroad@aol.com
www.essentialgenealogy.com

ISBN 10: 1-59360-163-8
ISBN 13: 978-159360-163-8
Library of Congress Control Number: 2012936571

PHOTO CREDITS

From flickr.com: front cover: yhoitink; back cover and page 7: Muffet.

Cover design by Matthew Simmons (www.myselfincluded.com). If you want to
contact the author directly, e-mail him at: wdanielquillen@gmail.com.

TABLE OF CONTENTS

MASTERING FAMILY, LIBRARY & CHURCH RECORDS

1. INTRODUCTION

Welcome! Welcome to *Mastering Family, Library & Church Records*. And, perhaps – welcome to the wonderful hobby / life sport called genealogy. I suppose it is a bit redundant to say that if you're not careful, genealogy will get into your blood. From the earliest generations of man on the earth, we have been interested in tracing our ancestors. Don't think so? Check out the number of genealogies that wend their way through the Bible, all the way back to Adam. As difficult as it must have been to keep records all those thousands of years ago, our forefathers did so, and we are fortunate to have them today.

Through the pages of this book, we'll focus on the kinds of records that will be available to you through your family, libraries of all kinds and churches. Some of the information doubtless will have occurred to you to search out, while other sources may be new to you. Many will be easy to find online, and others may take a little additional sleuthing to uncover. But all will provide resources for you to search out your ancestors.

Thank you for picking up this book. You may not be aware, but *Quillen's Essentials of Genealogy: Mastering Family, Library and Church Records* is the sixth in a series of other *Quillen's Essentials* books. One or more of the others may come in handy for your ancestral research:

• *Mastering Online Genealogy*
• *Mastering Immigration & Naturalization Records*

- *Mastering Census & Military Records*
- *Tracing Your European Roots*
- *Tracing Your Irish & British Roots*
- *Mastering Family, Library & Church Records*

While each of those books represents a focused dive into various areas of genealogical research, one of the first two genealogy books I wrote might also prove useful to you:

Secrets of Tracing Your Ancestors – This book was originally targeted at beginning genealogists, although reviewers have noted it contains sections, topics and tactics that are beneficial to beginning as well as more experienced researchers.

Troubleshooter's Guide to Do-It-Yourself Genealogy – This book is designed for genealogists with a little more experience in genealogical research, or perhaps those who have hit brick walls in their research and need a little extra help.

Cold Spring Press publishes all books in *The Quillen's Essentials of Genealogy* series as well as *Secrets* and the *Troubleshooter's Guide*.

As offered in all my books, if you run into difficulties, have questions, or just want to bounce something off me, you are welcome to e-mail me at *wdanielquillen@gmail.com*.

In addition, I have a website / blog at *www.essentialgenealogy.com*, which I invite you to check out. I frequently publish blog entries on various and sundry aspects of genealogy, and you may find answers or genealogical inspiration there.

INTRODUCTION

As I did in a number of my genealogy books, I will introduce you to my family. As we progress through the book, you'll get to know my family better, as I will use many of them to illustrate various aspects and methods of genealogical research.

I am William Daniel Quillen, and I am married to the lovely Bonita Blau. We have six children.

My parents are:
• William Edgar Quillen and Versie Lee Lowrance.

My grandparents were:
• Helon Edgar Quillen and Vivian Iris Cunningham.
• Elzie Lee Lowrance and Alma Hudson.

My great grandparents were:
• Edgar Estil Quillen and Theodora Charity McCollough
• William Edward Cunningham and Emma Adelia Sellers
• Thomas Newton Lowrance and Margaret Ann McClure
• Francis Marion Hudson and Margaret Ellen Turpin

My second great grandparents were:
• Jonathan Baldwin Quillen and Sarah Minerva Burke
• William Lindsay McCollough and Lucy Arabella Phillips
• William Huston Cunningham and Amanda Stunkard
• John Thomas Sellers and Celeste Elizabeth Horney
• Alpheus Marion Lowrance and Catherine Gemima Reece
• Jeremiah Hudson and Frances Duvall

My third great grandparents were:
• Charles Franklin Quillen and Susan or Susannah _____

- Samuel McCollough and Elizabeth Throckmorton
- Oliver Sayers Phillips and Charity Graham
- Joseph Cunningham and Sarah Rogers
- Matthew Stunkard and Margaret Peoples
- John T. Sellers and Elizabeth Ritchey
- Leonidas Horney and Jane Crawford
- Francis Marion Hudson and Mary Magdalene Yates
- John E. Duvall, Jr. and Elizabeth _____

My fourth great grandparents were:
- Levin Quillen and Priscilla Caudle
- Thomas McCollough and Sarah Dunn
- James Throckmorton and Jane Barclo
- John Phillips and Lydia Rutan
- George Graham, Jr. and Sallie Borman Mason

My fifth great grandparents were:
- John Quillin and _____
- Canada McCollough and Mary McFarland
- Job Throckmorton and Mary Morton
- George Graham Sr. and Charity Kimball
- James Mason and Mary Patterson

Now that you've met some of my family, let's learn a little more about the records available from your family, libraries, and churches!

2. THE BASICS

Before we get too far afield in tracing your ancestors, let's talk about some of the basics of genealogical research. Many of the hints and tips I put in my books are things I had to learn the hard way – in short, they are errors I made in the early days of my genealogical ramblings.

And ramblings they were. When I first started genealogy near the beginning of my third decade of life (i.e., in my early twenties!), I hadn't a clue what I was doing, how I should be doing it, and what I should be doing with valuable information once I obtained it. I made mistake after mistake, compounded by errors on top of miscues. I just had a vague sense of urgency and was undirected in my searching. Perhaps we can begin there: with Direction.

Direction

Before you aimlessly wander through genealogical records, in search of someone – anyone – who is a relative, you would be far better served to take a methodical, planned approach. Among other things, decide:

• Who you want to look for
• What you want to find (birth, death, marriage, children, parents, etc.)
• How much time and energy you want to spend on ancillary lines (your ancestor's wife's family, for instance)

Now, those admonitions may seem…silly. But if you do not begin with a goal in mind, I am here to tell you it will be very easy to find yourself spending time and energy in efforts that while good, are not the main purpose for your search. I have found it has been helpful to categorize my searches, or more particularly the information I find on those searches, as good, better, best:

- *Good* information is information that is related to my main goal, but that represents a tangent from the information I am really seeking.
- *Better* information is data that are more closely related to the goal I am seeking.
- *Best* information are facts that are immediately associated with the information I am seeking, if not the very information I am seeking.

Let me give you an example. Several years ago I was trying (once again!) to determine the birth location of my second great grandfather, Jonathan Baldwin Quillen. I had traced him to a small town in south central Missouri – Hartville, Wright County, Missouri. For years, I have been searching for his exact birth date and place of birth, but to no avail. Most (but not all!) of the records and information I have is that he was born in Tennessee, and I have a number of supposed birthdates, only one (or none) of which can be correct. It occurred to me that his death certificate might provide me with the information I was seeking. So off to Wright County, Missouri records I went.

As I poked and prodded around in Wright County, I was unable to find a death certificate for Jonathan. I did, however, find his obituary:

J. B. Quillen died January 21, 1920, aged 74 years, 8 months, and 3 days.

He had been in poor health for two years and bore his suffering with patience and said the Lord was with him in his last hours and that he was willing and ready to go. Everything was done for him that willing hands could do. We will miss our dear grandfather, but our loss is Heaven's gain.

He leaves an aged widow and seven children to mourn his loss. The remains were laid to rest in the Curtis Cemetery eight miles south of Hartville last Thursday.

Dearest father, thou hast left us here,
Thy loss we deeply feel
But 'tis God that hath bereft us
He can all our sorrows heal.
Peacefully we know you're resting,
In that home so bright and fair,
And we know when life is ended,
We will meet our father there.

– Marie Hensley

Based on information from his obituary, my search for his death certificate led me to the Curtis Cemetery, south of Hartville. In no time at all, I found the grave of his infant grandson, who was buried in the same cemetery as his grandpa. That led me to the grandson's mother's grave, which included her maiden name – Coday. I then found a bevy of Coday family members buried in Curtis cemetery. I found myself tracking and recording this information for the Codays – many of them. I spent hours and hours recording details about the Coday family.

Because I lost my focus, I allowed myself to be distracted from my true goal – finding my second great grandfather's birth date and / or place. From a good, better, best scenario, here is what my hours of research yielded:

• Good – I was able to capture a great deal of information about a goodly number of Codays, one of whom had married into my family.

- Better – I was able to locate the grave and death certificate for one of my second great grandfather's grandsons, as well as his son's grave.
- Best – I am still searching for my second great grandfather's birth information.

It would have been better to simply make a note that there were a number of Coday family members buried in the Curtis Cemetery in Wright County, Missouri, and that their death certificates could be found on the vital records website hosted by the state of Missouri. Recording that information would have taken minutes, and I could return at a future date and spend time gathering the Codays when I had time to do so, when they were the primary goal of my search.

In *Secrets of Tracing Your Ancestors*, I provide a *Research Log* to assist with your research. Had I been using this log as part of my search for Jonathan's birth information, perhaps I wouldn't have gotten so easily distracted. I have included a copy of the *Research Log* on the next page, but you can also download it from my genealogy website – *www.essentialgenealogy.com*. Or, if you prefer, I can e-mail you a Word copy of the form.

Without such a log, unless you have iron will power and terrific focus, you may find yourself spending precious hours running down semi-related genealogical threads, but ignoring your main purpose. It's sort of like the person who lives their lives through checklists. Don't get me wrong — checklists can be good, but they can also give the illusion of progress, when the progress itself is just completing the checklist.

Okay – so I hope I haven't offended all you checklist aficionados out there! But I think you get my point.

RESEARCH LOG

Ancestor's Given Name(s): EDGAR ESTIL   Last name: QUILLEN   Page 1 of __

Research Objective: FIND GRANDPA ED'S BIRTHDATE. HE ALWAYS SAID HE WAS BORN 15 JAN 1880, BUT THE 1880 CENSUS (WHICH WAS TAKEN JUNE 1, 1880) LISTS EVERYONE IN HIS FAMILY - EXCEPT HIM! SO I THINK HE MAY HAVE BEEN BORN AFTER THE CENSUS WAS TAKEN. MAYBE 1881?

Date of Search	Source:	Comments
9 Dec 1998	1880 LEE CO. VIRGINIA CENSUS	ALL MEMBERS OF THE FAMILY ARE LISTED - EXCEPT ED. CENSUS DATE: 1 JUNE 1880
3 Aug 1999	LEE COUNTY, VA RECORDS BOOK IN GATE CITY, VIRGINIA.	GRANDPA ED'S BURIAL RECORDS ARE NOT RECORDED, ALTHOUGH HIS BROTHERS AND SISTERS ARE.
16 Aug 1999	VIRGINIA STATE LIBRARY - VITAL STATISTICS SECTION	WENT THROUGH 20 YEARS OF BIRTH RECORDS FOR LEE COUNTY AND THERE IS NO RECORD OF HIS BIRTH.
7 JAN 2001	FAMILYSEARCH.ORG.	CHECKED VARIOUS RECORD COLLECTIONS ON FAMILYSEARCH, BUT THERE WERE NO RECORDS OF HIS BIRTH THERE!

Don't get distracted! Stay on the main hunt.

Citing Sources

Oh that I had received and followed this advice early in my genealogical career. Amazingly, I actually remember thinking on more than one occasion:

"I should write down where I got this information. Oh – no need – this is important enough, I will be able to remember where I got it."

I have lived to rue that day (those days)! So much of the genealogy work I did several decades ago was done in genealogy libraries, censuses, books, and countless other sources without the aid of indexes or the Internet. I have great gobs of information which now has no citation information whatsoever. While it is a clue for me to search for the source again and identify it, it is not the same as having identified my source in the first place.

Why is it critical to cite your sources, and cite them properly? The answer is not so you will get a passing grade in Mrs. Johnson's freshman English class for your term paper (although that should almost be reason enough!). It is so you can separate out the information you know from primary sources of information, versus information you have discovered through secondary sources of information. (More on primary and secondary sources shortly.) I suspect you can come up with your own list of things critical to successful source citation. Here are a few areas that come to my mind:

• Author / source
• Title of source
• Publisher
• Where in source information appeared (if applicable)

• Location of source

• Internet citation

Let's cover each of these items:

Author / source – You should identify the author of the source. If it is a book, list the author's name. If it is family tradition, write down who told it to you and when. For example, my great aunt Ruth was for years a wonderful source of genealogical information for me. None of her information was recorded, but she knew all the family stories, dates, etc.

Title – If your source is a book, list the title of the book. It might be a formal title, like one family history I have: *Cousins by the Dozens: The Sellers Family in America*. Or, it may be the title of a government-held record. For example, I located the record of my second great grandparents' marriage in a county office in a volume entitled: *Lee County, Virginia Marriage Register, Volume 3*.

Publisher – if your source is a book, be sure and include this information, usually found in the front pages of the book. If the book is out of print, you may be able to contact the publisher to see if they have any additional copies, or they can put you in touch with the author who may order additional copies to be printed. You should also include the date the book was published, and if there are multiple editions, list the edition number. If an ISBN number is available, include that also.

Where source information appeared – If the source is a book, include the page number where the information was found. I have a peculiar page number identification method; not only do I list the page number, but I indicate the approximate area of the page where the information was located. For example, page 113b tells me the information was located about half way down on page 113 (I use a, b and c to identify location on the page). If there are two columns, and the information is in the second column, about the middle of the column, it would be listed as page 113e – column 1 is 113a, 113b and 113c, and column two is page 113d, 113e and 113f. If your source is a website, then identify what tab or where on the page the information is listed.

Location of source – Identify where you found your source. What was the library, website, county courthouse where the information was located? A special note about censuses: If you do much genealogical research in the United States between 1850 and 1940, you are likely to peruse censuses in your research. Here is a typical census annotation I have used:

> **Census year:** 1870 **Territory:** Illinois **County:** Schuyler **Division:** Littleton **Township Reel number:** M593-276, **Page number:** 143a **Reference:** Enumerated by James DeWitt the 23rd of June 1870

You'll note this annotation included a microfilm reel number. At the time I was researching this family, indexes for the 1870 census were not yet developed, so this was a must to have. I could find the information again without poring over microfilm page after microfilm page of the census.

Internet citation – with the ubiquitous nature of the Internet, and the proliferation of genealogical information now available there, you will certainly be finding information on the Internet. Be sure and write down the URL (address) of the website.

Dead-end Websites

Every now and then, you are likely to find a link to a website you will be very excited about. With great anticipation, you click on the website, only to be confronted with this rather rude Internet message (referred to as a *Google*

404 message) that says: "**This page cannot be found.** The page you are looking for might have been removed, had its name changed, or is temporarily unavailable."

If you run into such a boorish message, don't dismay – there are options available that may save the day. Certainly don't feel picked on – websites routinely come and go, and if you ran into this error message, you found a website that must be out on a walk about.

Your first step is to begin at the end of the website address. Begin by trimming it back a small section at a time. If you do that, you may find that an internal link has changed, and by moving backwards on the address, you can get to one of the main pages for the website, from where you can then search for the information that was not accessible. This often works for me.

If that doesn't work, then *Google cache* is a great alternative. Return to the main Google page where you found the link. At the end of the summary of the link, you will most likely see the term *Cached*. Google takes a snapshot of every page it locates, and stores (caches) that snapshot. If you click on the word *Cached*, you'll be taken to the archived page as saved by Google. That may solve your mystery – even for links that have been taken down, this is a way you can locate it.

> Don't panic if you find a "broken" or non-functioning website! There are options available!

In case that doesn't work for you, I have one more option to try. Go first to *www.archive.org*. In the middle-center of the page, you'll see the words *Wayback Machine*, along with a window in which you can place the URL (the website address with which you are having difficulty), then click on the button that says: *Take me back*. (Note the window on the Wayback

Machine already supplies the http:// portion of the website; don't re-enter that part of the URL.) You'll be taken to a rather large calendar, full of years and months of the year. If your website was archived, you should see the dates on which that happened. If you'll click on one of the highlighted dates, you should be taken back to the website on the date it appeared. It is a slick tool to know about and use when you run into roadblocks on the Internet.

I could also combine several of the search options mentioned here to find the website for which I am looking. If I had gotten an error message in the *Wayback Machine*, I could have trimmed back several sections of the URL, until I get one that works for me, and from where I might proceed to the actual page I am seeking.

Primary & Secondary Sources of Information
Primary sources of information include information recorded at the time of the event. A government- or hospital-issued birth certificate, for example, is considered a primary source of information. A death certificate listing the date of death and burial is also considered a primary source of information. A secondary source of information is information recorded some time after the event. I mentioned earlier that a death certificate is considered a primary source of death and burial information. It is, however, considered a secondary source for birth information, if such is listed on the death certificate. Why? Because it may be 80-plus years since the individual's birth that the information is being provided, and that by someone who was not there at the time – his wife, one of his children, etc. Errors that had crept in through the years – either by design or by accident – are perpetuated.

If my grandfather, Elzie Lee Lowrance, ever had a birth certificate, it has been lost long ago. I do, however, have a document called an *Affidavit of Live Birth* – a document signed by his parents affirming my grandfather's birth on a certain date in a certain place. Would that document be considered a primary or secondary source of information? I would say it is a secondary source. Yes, at least my grandfather's mother was present at the time of his birth, perhaps even my grandfather. But – it may have been several decades earlier that my grandfather's birth occurred. His mother may get his birthdate confused with one of his siblings. Or – and this is a possibility, perhaps the *affidavit* lists his birth date as a year or two later than it is to keep him out of military service. Or – perhaps it lists his birth date earlier than it really is so that he is of legal age to marry.

Organization

A few years ago, I realized I was gleaning a ton of genealogical information on a number of my family lines, and it wasn't organized very well. Stacks of papers, filing cabinets full of papers. "Now where is Grandma Dollie's information? Do I have all her information in with her husband, or with her father?" I decided I needed to organize my genealogy information.

> **Do what it takes to find primary sources of information.**

The advent of genealogy software has been a great boon to genealogists everywhere! With a few clicks of a mouse, I can store genealogical data and keep it for years and years. (Be sure and back up your genealogy software, by the way!)

But what about paper records? With today's technology, I can certainly scan original birth, death and marriage certificates, draft registration cards, even census pages and ship passenger lists. But what do I do with the paper copies? In *Secrets of Tracing Your Ancestors*, I spend quite a bit of time identifying the filing system I created and continue to us for keeping hard copies of birth and death certificates, marriage certificates2, etc.

I am fortunate enough to have the original center section of my great grandmother's Bible. It contains the generations of her husband and herself back to the late 1700s, including the names and genealogical information on nearly 500 of my ancestors. You can see how I would want to preserve and protect such a document. My great grandmother, Emma Adelia Sellers, died in 1943 just prior to her 75th birthday. At a minimum the document is at least 80 years old, and I would estimate closer to 100 years old. It is one of my most prized genealogical possessions, and is something I want to protect. To prevent wear and tear on the document, I carefully photocopied it, and use the photocopy for my genealogical work. I store the original in a safe place.

In *Secrets of Tracing Your Ancestors*, I lay out my organizational plan for paper documents. The foundation of my filing system is the surname file. For example, in the first chapter, I introduced you to my family. Surname files have been set up for each of those surnames:

Burke

Crawford

Cunningham

Graham

Duvall

Horney

Hudson

Lowrance

McClure

McCollough

Peoples

Phillips

Quillen

Reece

Ritchey

Rogers
Sellers
Stunkard
Throckmorton
Turpin

Within each file are manila folders that are labeled *Birth Records, Marriage Records, Death Records*, and so forth. As I receive those kinds of records, I copy them and put them in each of the appropriate surname files. Theodora Charity McCollough is my great grandmother, and she married Edgar Estil Quillen. Information about her birth is contained in the McCollough surname file (since at birth she was a McCollough), but her death certificate is contained in the Quillen file, because that was her name when she passed away.

Death certificates are often found in two places – in birth as well as death files, because they often contain information about an individual's birth. As you run across other records and need additional manila folders – add them! You probably don't need *Military Records* or *Immigration and Naturalization* folders for all of your surname files, but for those that do, create them. If you find records you just don't know where to file (divorce records, criminal records(!), probate records, land records), you can either put them in a *Miscellaneous* file or create a separate file for them.

I include in these files information that might not be in a hard-copy format. For example, if my great aunt Ruth told me my Aunt Agnes was born in Cottonwood Falls, Kansas (she did!), then I will simply write or type it on a piece of paper and file it under Aunt Agnes's birth file to make certain I do not lose track of the information.

So – in a nutshell, that's my organizational system for paper records. Please feel free to modify and improve upon it – it just needs to work for you.

3. MASTERING FAMILY RECORDS

I once attended a genealogy conference at Brigham Young University in Provo, Utah. It was a wonderful conference, one from which I gleaned a lot of information and inspiration. The title of one of the break-out sessions was something like: *Bottom Left-Hand-Drawer Genealogy*. The point of the speaker's entire presentation was that you mustn't overlook information that might be at your (or someone else's) very fingertips, crammed in a forgotten drawer, slipped into an unmarked shoe box in the top corner of the closet, etc.

I couldn't agree more! For years, I visited my grandparents every summer in Oklahoma. At the back of their yard was a smallish structure – a garage in former days, I suppose, but used for many years to house lawn mowers, Christmas decorations, tools, clothes packed in boxes decades before and stored in the rafters, etc.

Upon my grandmother's death, my parents drove to Oklahoma to help my grandfather clean everything out of the house and "garage," and get his home ready to sell, as he planned to move to Colorado and live with my folks.

In a dark and musty corner of the garage, they discovered a box, covered in probably forty years of dirt and grime, cobwebs and mildew. Inside the box were over 400 pictures of my ancestors! Some of the pictures were of ancestors who had died in the mid-1800s. They had apparently been the possessions of my great grandmother (Emma Adelia Sellers), the one who had also kept the genealogy we found in the center section of the family Bible. On the backs of probably 80% of the pictures was a description of those who were in the picture along with the date of the picture (at least the year), written in Emma's lovely hand. What a treasure.

Using the genealogy Emma had penned as well as her writings on the backs of the pictures, I was able to piece together scores of families, and put faces to names of ancestors that would otherwise have been long lost.

Ah, but you say you haven't got grandparents living in Oklahoma with an old garage that houses family photographs. While that may be true, *someone* in the family may be the repository of such genealogical treasures, along with other important and critical documents precious to genealogists. Your mission, should you choose to accept it, is to locate that person and get copies of all those items.

Begin at Home
Before we get too far ahead of ourselves, let's slow down and start at the beginning. As you begin your research, begin at home. And I'm not necessarily talking about beginning in your parents' home, but beginning in your own home. Someday, if not already, you will have children and grandchildren who will be interested in your life. Be sure and provide for them those very documents you so covetously seek for your ancestors: your birth certificate, marriage certificate, and other formal certificates that document important events in your life. As the presenter at the genealogy conference addressed, pull out those documents and make copies of them for your genealogical story.

Birth certificates are especially valuable for genealogical purposes. They serve as primary sources of documentation for the individual featured thereon:

- birth date and place;
- full names of father and mother;
- parents' address;
- often, parents' birthplaces;
- occasionally, parents' occupations.

Again – none of this information should be new to you, but it may well be of interest to your posterity, especially a descendant that has as much interest in genealogy as you do.

You're married? Wouldn't it be nice to provide a copy of your marriage certificate as part of your life's story? Your sweetheart will want a mention in the story of your life. And, if you've done much genealogical research, you know that women's maiden names are often lost to history, and they become Mrs. So-and-So. Providing a copy of your marriage certificate ensures your or your spouse's maiden name is preserved. Typically, marriage certificates will include the names of the wedding party, including bride and groom, often the parents of both, and the names of witnesses to the wedding – often relatives (typically fathers, grandfathers or brothers and sisters).

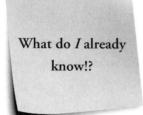

What do *I* already know!?

Look beyond yourself

After gathering all the information about yourself, your spouse and your children, it's time to begin climbing the family tree. You should search out and record all the information you know about your immediate progenitors – your parents, grandparents, siblings, etc. It may surprise you how much information you already know. Be sure and capture that information – in genealogy software, books, etc.

Record the information you already know – your parents' birth dates and places, their marriage information and if applicable, their death information. Gather the same information for each of your siblings as well. Unless you are absolutely certain of the veracity of the information, confirm it with those who are still living. Do all you can to collect copies of the documents that confirm the information: birth certificates, marriage certificates, death certificates, etc.

In *Secrets of Tracing Your Ancestors*, I mention that most genealogists suggest you begin with your parents when searching for your ancestors. While I agree that is sound counsel in general, I think there is at least one other person you should first start with: your Aunt Ruth.

My experience tells me that an amazing number of families have an Aunt Ruth. Aunt Ruth is the elderly relative that seems to have collected all the family history and lore. For some reason, she has shown an intense interest in the family, and all the family information and history has found its way to her. (In fact, since you have this book, you may be Aunt Ruth, or will be as you age!)

My Aunt Ruth was my grandfather's younger sister. An Oklahoma widow for many years, she was a constant source of information about the family: why Uncle Clint was called Bud, why the Jonathan Baldwin Quillen family left Virginia after their family had lived there several hundred years, etc. I was always amazed that Ruth seemed to know a little (or a lot!) about virtually any family member about whom I had queries.

And so – due to her advancing age – my suggestion is you begin with your Aunt Ruth. Before you even begin with your parents, find out what your Aunt Ruth knows, especially if she is older than your parents. Get to her and reap her memories and knowledge about the family before she goes to join those long-departed ancestors about whom she knew so much.

Arrange to sit down with your Aunt Ruth – visit if necessary – to discuss what she knows about the family. First of all, she'll likely enjoy your visit, and secondly, she'll especially enjoy speaking about the family. Her joy and love of the family are what have prompted her to gather all the family history.

Before you visit your Aunt Ruth, plan your visit: determine what you want to know about whom. What information is most necessary for you to find out, and what information is she likely to be able to supply? Here are some questions you might consider asking her:

• What was your father's full name? Did he use any nicknames?
• Where was he born?
• When was he born (at least the year)?
• Did he ever leave his hometown? If so, where did he go, and why?
• What did he do for a living?
• Was he ever in the military?
• What were his parents' names? Where were they from? Do you remember his mother's maiden name?
• Did he have any siblings? How many? Was he the oldest, youngest, in the middle?
• Do you know the names of his siblings? How about their ages? (Was Aunt Susie two years younger than your dad?)
• What did he look like? Do you have any pictures of him? Who would have some if you don't?

And don't forget these kinds of questions:

• What are your favorite recollections of him?
• Did he have a sense of humor? Or a hot temper (that runs in my family!)?
• Did he love animals?
• What did he do for fun and relaxation?

•What do you miss most about him?

•What are some of your favorite stories from his life?

When interviewing your Aunt Ruth, pretend you are in school. Date your paper. Put your name on it. Write down who you are interviewing. You may think you'll always remember those things, but after a few years the specifics will fade, I guarantee you.

My editor once gave me the key to being a successful travel guide writer, and I think it applies to genealogists too, especially as it relates to interviewing relatives. He said, "You must be curious. Don't just get the facts, get the facts behind the facts." So – be curious.

Be sure and ask for maiden names, nicknames and pet names. My great grandmother's name was Theodora Charity McCollough, but everyone called her Dolly. And her mother was called Grandma Mac.

I think I did a pretty good job of gleaning information from my Aunt Ruth. She always expressed appreciation for my visits (and often asked me to come again!) and happily shared information about family members in whom I was interested. And yet, now that she has passed, I often think of information I wish I had thought to ask her about. I ventured those same questions to her daughters, and the answer was always the same: "Oh, I'm sorry – I just don't know. Momma would have known, but I just don't know."

As wonderful a resource as Aunt Ruths may be, they come with a caveat: be cautious of the information they provide you, and do not take it as the Gospel Truth. I learned that lesson the hard way. I had asked her where her uncle's

Who is *my* Aunt Ruth?

wife was born and she told me Cottonwood Falls, Kansas. For years I followed that thread and could never find her birth certificate in Cottonwood Falls. Then quite by accident I found information that indicated she was actually born several counties away in Sharon Springs, Kansas. Checking out the clue, I was rewarded with success, but not before I had wandered around several hundred miles away from my goal – her birth certificate. My Aunt Ruth got me close, however.

Lest you think my Aunt Ruth's information couldn't be trusted, I'll share one more bit of information she shared. She spoke of one of my second great grandmothers. She it was who let me know that this particular relative was embarrassed that she was born in Texas, so she told everyone she was born in Arkansas. As I researched her life, I found her in censuses as a young and then older married woman. Her birth place was given as Arkansas. However, when I finally found her maiden name, and then her parents' names, I was able to find that family in the census. Sure enough – her birth place was listed as Texas! (Thanks, Ruth, and – sorry to my Lonestar State readers!)

Ask your Aunt Ruth if she has any documents about family members. Often, other family members know of Ruth's interest in the family, and documents just seem to find their way to her. For example, my Aunt Ruth had her parents' marriage certificate, as well as their death certificates. She had two family histories written about two lines of our family – the Grahams and Throckmortons. As a youth I thought these were cool, because my grandfather's name was included in each of the books. Prior to her death, knowing my love of the family and genealogy, my Aunt Ruth indicated I should receive both these books upon her death, and they are now in my possession.

Don't limit yourself to government documents (birth, marriage and death certificates) or family histories. Sometimes, old letters can shed tremendous light on the family. To today's generation, it may seem odd that people used to keep letters from loved ones. But often, those scraps of paper were all some family members had of a sister, or parent, who lived far away. Today, we think nothing of hopping on a plane or jumping in the car to visit a distant relative. Such was not the case just two generations ago. Often, when a daughter married and moved across country, she bid adieu to parents, siblings, etc., never to see them again. Letters were precious connections to these loved ones, and they were often saved.

I have a number of family letters my great grandmother Emma Adelia saved. One was a sad tome – she had gone to spend time with a beloved sister who was dying of diabetes-related health problems, and my great grandmother was briefing her brother on many aspects of the visit. She spoke about her sister's battle, her brother-in-law's efforts to keep her comfortable and the struggle he was having with her impending death. She spoke about the children and their reactions to their mother's passing. From the letter, I learned:

•her sister's name
•her brother's name
•her sister's husband's name
•the names of all of her sister's children
•the date of her sister's death
•the place of her sister's death
•the cause of her sister's death
•at the time of her sister's death, their parents lived in the same town where she lived.

In addition to these important facts, I got a peek into my great grandmother's heart and soul. I almost feel the pain she felt as she described her sister's suffering. I felt the great love she had for this sister and for her sister's family.

Nearby relatives

One effective tactic you can use when you run into a brick wall on a particular ancestor is to scour the areas surrounding your ancestor's last known place of residence. Often, there will be descendants still living in the area, who may already know the information you are seeking, have the documents you would like copies of, etc.

A few years ago, I was perusing a family genealogy I have of the Throckmorton family. It was published in 1929, and is a wonderful, 400+ page book with information about that family and many of the people who married into the family. As I was flipping through the pages, I came across a photo of the old Throckmorton family Bible. The photo was of the center section of the family Bible, which contained names of family members and their critical information – birth, marriage and death dates, etc. I got to wondering where that Bible was, and if I could contact the owner and get copies of those pages from the Bible.

Look up relatives that live near where my ancestors lived.

Even though the photo of the Bible had been taken in 1929 (at the latest), I was hopeful the Bible had been kept in the family and handed down from generation to generation, recognized as a precious family heirloom. I went to the Internet to see if I could find any Throckmortons living in the small Pennsylvania town from which many of the Throckmortons came. Success! There were a goodly number living in the area. So, I began calling them, one by one. The first few calls were answered by individuals who were very pleasant, although they didn't know anything about the Bible. Finally, I spoke with a woman – a very distant cousin – who thought the Bible might be in the possession of old Aunt So-and-So's family (sorry – I cannot recall Aunt So-and-So's real name). I got in touch with the family and…nothing. A dead end. Seems one or two of the people I spoke with in that family vaguely remembered seeing the Bible, but that had been years before, and they just didn't know who had it now. Sigh…sometimes your searches end (at least temporarily) that way.

However, just writing about it has encouraged me to reach out again and repeat my search (unfortunately I didn't write down the names of those with whom I had spoken) to see if I can't find this great genealogical asset. I'll update this story in future editions.

I suspect this tactic works best for unique surnames: Quillen, Cunningham, Sellers, Throckmorton, Horney, etc. It would be tough to do if you are researching surnames like Miller, Smith, Jones, etc!

But hopefully, my Throckmorton Bible story serves to encourage you to try the same tactic yourself. Can't find your great grandfather Snodgrass's birth date, but you know he was from Podunk, Iowa? Then check out the good folks in Podunk and see if there are any Snodgrasses still living there. If not there, perhaps they are in a nearby town, or elsewhere in the state. It's certainly worth the effort. You may run across long-lost cousins you knew nothing about and may even get the information you are seeking.

If the ancestor for whom you are searching lived in several different locales, don't limit your searches for fellow family members to only one place – check all the places he lived. For example, my great grandfather Edgar Estil Quillen lived near Estillville, Virginia as a child and young adolescent. Then, when he was about 16, his family moved to Hartville, Missouri. Shortly after his marriage, he moved outside Ralston, Oklahoma. Now – I happen to know a lot about him and his family (in fact, his daughter Ruth is the Aunt Ruth I mentioned so lovingly earlier in this chapter). But if I didn't know much about him, I would check for Quillens living in Estillville (now Gate City), Hartville and Ralston to see if any of them knew anything about my great grandfather or any of his family.

During the 17th, 18th and 19th centuries, families often had many children. Even though one or more members of your family pulled up stakes and moved elsewhere, they may have left behind parents, siblings, aunts, uncles or other family members whose descendants still live in the area and may be of assistance to you in your search for common ancestors. Even though someone was your ancestor's cousin, and is now your very extended cousin, that cousin and your ancestor shared the same grandparents – and maybe a genealogist or two has sprung up in that branch of the family in the ensuing generations. It's certainly worth a little Internet research and few phone calls.

Family reunions

I have had great success making connections and furthering my genealogical efforts through attendance at family reunions, and they may provide another arrow in your genealogical quiver.

As I began my genealogical journey over three decades ago, I learned that my great grandfather, Edgar Estil Quillen, was from Estillville, Lee County Virginia. It seems that the main branches of the Quillen clan in America set up house and shop for over 300 years near the confluence of the states of Virginia, Kentucky, Tennessee and North Carolina. Subsequently, I have learned that those areas are still heavily populated with members of the Quillen clan.

In the early days of my genealogical research, I discovered the Quillen family held a reunion the fourth Sunday of every August at a church near Gate City, Virginia. Since I was a poor college student at the time, living in Utah, I tucked that information away for a time when I had time and money to go. About ten years later I found myself living in New Jersey, so figured out a way to be in the Gate City area on the fourth Sunday of August. And I am glad I did.

Sometime during the past 100 years, some Quillen who was hoping for Brownie points in heaven (no doubt) gave some land to the local Baptist church with the stipulation that the church allow the Quillen clan to have a reunion in any building built there on the fourth Sunday of every August. So that bright summer's day in about 1987, found me entering an old Baptist church, one of about 100 Quillens attending the reunion. It was a delightful experience. I was able to meet family members and establish a few genealogical connections.

LOST QUILLEN!

While attending a Quillen family reunion in Gate City, Virginia, many years ago, I stood to introduce myself at the beginning of the reunion. I explained that my great grandfather and his family left Gate City in the late 1880s, headed for the west. I explained that since they had been gone for so long (100 years at that point), I wasn't certain exactly how I fit into the family that was gathered there.

One older gentleman took pity on me. He took me by the arm and guided me to clumps of Quillens, introducing me as the "lost Quillen."

When he introduced me as the lost Quillen to a spry septuagenarian, the elderly gent squinted up at me and said, "Lost, huh? Then you must be a Democrat!" Turns out the elderly Quillen was Senator Jimmy Quillen, Republican US Senator from Tennessee for 34 years!

My grandmother was Alma Hudson Lowrance. Many of the Hudsons seem to be prolific genealogists, and their nation-wide family reunions have one focus – genealogy. When you go to this family reunion, you'd better know what your heritage is, and be prepared to discuss it, and help others along their genealogical line.

But, you ask, where can you find out about family reunions? Well, keep your ears open. I originally learned about the Quillen family reunion from a fellow genealogist, a woman who gladly shared her knowledge about the family with me when I was just starting out. Or – join a family association – they will often have family reunions / gatherings. That's how I learned about the Hudson reunion – it was announced in the Hudson Family Association's newsletter.

Many family groups are entering the 21st century and getting Facebook pages. That is also a great place to find out about family reunions. Message boards will also have information about upcoming family reunions.

And – don't forget the good ol' Internet when it comes to finding out about family reunions. Just go to Google and search: Quillen family reunion, Throckmorton family reunion, Snodgrass family reunion, etc. While writing this book, I went to the Internet and typed *Quillen family reunion.* Sure enough – I found a number of hits that spoke about the Quillen family reunion in Gate City – the one I mentioned above. There were several newspaper articles about previous reunions, announcements about the upcoming reunion, etc. One of the newspaper hits I found included an article announcing the 2006 reunion:

> Quillin and Quillen family reunion will be held August 20 at the Antioch Church, Highway 71, Gate City, VA. Call (423) 378-3522.

(I showed the real telephone number in case any Quillens are reading this book that want to get more information about the reunion!) So don't shy away from those family reunions.

Facebook

I mentioned Facebook above, and thought I would take a minute or two and share a few thoughts about it as it pertains to ancestral searches. You can now list surname groups on Facebook, and this is a great way to interact with a bevy of individuals who share your surname, or interest therein. I have friends and fellow genealogists who have shared great genealogical successes they have had as they have connected with other researchers and family members via Facebook.

There are several ways to find the Facebook page for your surname. The first is to go onto Facebook itself. From about any of the pages you are at on Facebook, look for the search box that says *Search for people, places or things*. From there you type (Surname) family – Quillen family, Throckmorton family, etc, and see what comes up.

You can also go to the Internet and Google it by typing something like: Quillen Facebook page. You'll get a lot of first-and-last-name Quillen Facebook pages, so you may have to weed through them until you find a generic Facebook page for your surname. You can try using Boolean operators like quotations along with the word *and*: "Quillen Facebook" and genealogy. Following are the hits I got by trying several variations:

• Quillen Facebook page — 507,000 hits
• "Quillen Facebook" — 2,590 hits (slightly more manageable)
• "Quillen Facebook" and genealogy – 207 hits (even better!)

Even though many in that last group are still the individual Facebook pages of individuals, many of them mention the individual is an avid genealogist, is looking for genealogy information, etc. They would be a great family connection to make.

It's certainly worth the effort to try the cyber-social network angle to finding your ancestors!

Journals &Autobiographies

I think two often-overlooked areas of genealogy are journals and autobiographies – your life story. One is a micro view of your life (your journals), while the other is a macro view (autobiography). Can you imagine the genealogical joy you would have if you stumbled across a journal or an autobiography written by some long-lost ancestor? Oh the things you could learn about them, their lives, their loves, their triumphs and tragedies! Let's take each of these in turn.

Every so often I teach beginning genealogy classes. To introduce one of the sessions, I bring in a book I claim is my third great grandfather's journal. It is a wonderful old tome: about 11"x14", with old worn leather and yellowing pages. Before I share its contents, we discuss as a class the wonderful things we might find in the journal – his life, loves, triumphs, tragedies. The everyday dealings of his life. After a good discussion, I open the journal and display…nothing! What a loss! What he could have written that would have opened his life to me had he only kept a journal.

With that object lesson in mind, we discuss the importance of keeping a journal, and the value it would provide to your descendants.

My wife and I have kept journals for about forty years. They are wonderful volumes filled with details about our lives. We have a tradition in our family called *High Chair*, which we followed religiously when our children were growing up (they have all left the house now). On each family member's birthday, after dinner, we gathered in our family room to honor that family member. The honoree sat in a wonderful old rocking chair we have, and then each family member would share reasons why they love and admire that person. After we had gone around the family several times, then my wife and I would share our journal entries about that child from the day they were born. Even though the children have heard their story many times, they still look forward to hearing about it during High Chair.

(Note: now that our kids are grown and gone from our home, we continue the High Chair tradition virtually via a blog.)

In addition to what's going on in our lives, at the beginning of each year, I take time to write a bit about our family – sort of a *State of the Quillen Family* entry. I include information about what each family member is up to, information about my job and salary, where we are living, the value of our home, cost of our mortgage, and then costs of things like a loaf of bread, pound of hamburger, gallon of milk, etc. It's already fascinating to look back to the beginning days of our marriage and smile about the sheer fear we had as we stepped up to a $356 monthly mortgage on our first home! Of course, I was only making $15,000 at the time, but still….

After all is said and done about my journal writing, my wife doesn't like my journal. First of all, she thinks I don't write often enough. But that's not all. On occasion, she will read a journal entry of mine, and her response is usually: "Where's the emotion? How did you feel about that? It's just the facts!"

Just the facts, Ma'am. That's me, I am afraid. And yet, I think facts are also parts of journals. As a teenager, I ran across a few pages of a budget my mother had kept when she and my father were first married (1951). Budget items included $10 a month for rent, $2 for utilities, etc. It was astounding to me, and I suspect that was what drove me to begin sharing similar things in my journal.

But I have to admit, there aren't usually many feelings or emotions in my journal entries. I mentioned an important and favorite part of High Chair with our kids was listening to their mother and me read from our journals about the day of their birth. My wife's entries are filled with her thoughts and feelings about these precious little spirits that had joined our family. My entries generally indicated their weight and length, the precise time they were born, whether or not they had hair (no), and — what the weather was like on the day they were born. Just the facts.

About a year ago, through partnership with one of my favorite genealogy societies, I received a transcription and photocopy of the *Day Book* (journal) of my third great grandfather, Leonidas Horney. When he was a young man, he joined the Illinois militia and fought in the Mexican American War. He kept his Day Book while marching, riding and sailing to and fighting in Mexico. I was so excited to read it and learn more about this ancestral hero of mine.

Alas — it was...just the facts. (Imagine that!)

He kept the journal only for the first part of his service: from July 22, 1846 to September 26, 1846. Two months in the life of this 29-year-old military ancestor of mine. Included in the pages are many weather-related entries ("Cool wind from the north," and "...some days cool all day..."), how many deer they saw and killed when they hunted for their Company, the names of four fellow soldiers and the amount of money lent to them, the size of grape vines he saw, the high costs he encountered in San Antonio during his trek: corn ($1 a bushel), whiskey (10 cents per drink), 25 cents for a small apple pie, $1 a gallon for molasses. He also took the time to notate the miles they marched or sailed between points.

Just the facts.

Sigh...so at least I get it honest — now I know my fact-based writing is genetic!

He did describe some of the women he saw in San Antonio:

> Some few of the Mexican women are very handsome but are mostly the rechedest things that could be immagined, especialy the old ones.

Someone had (thankfully!) transcribed his journal (he and I share poor handwriting). There was a bit or irony in his journal of which he would never be aware. On July 22, 1846, one of his mileage entries read:

> 400 (miles) from Memphis to Vicksburgh
> 350 (miles) from Vicksburgh to Natches

Just shy of seventeen years later, on May 16, 1863, Leonidas Horney was killed at a battle that was part of the siege of Vicksburg — Champion Hill. What did I learn from this experience? Well, I have decided to try and put a little more feeling into my journal writing, more introspection and thoughts about events. I'll try to keep in mind that some distant descendant of mine might like to know what I thought about life and all that swirls around it.

Now, if you haven't kept a journal your entire life, don't fret – just start now. If you are 40, 50, 60 or even older, that's okay. Start now. As far as I know, my grandfather never kept a journal – until my grandmother contracted cancer. That day, he began keeping a journal. It lasted for only two years, until his last entry: "Vivian has gone home to that God who gave her life." While it is not an extensive journal, it is still precious to me.

Start / keep a journal!

Autobiography / Life Story

I am a realist – I know the lives of most of us today are so busy. But if you make this a priority, and set aside a regular time to write your life story, it can be done. At one of the busiest times of my life, I undertook to write my life story. I decided that once a month, I could spend a few hours on my life story by writing a few hours after church instead of coming home and taking a nap. So the first Sunday of every month that's what I did. Now, that isn't much time, but after a year of that – maybe 24 or 36 hours of writing – my life story began to take shape.

I started by laying out my *Table of Contents*. Then I entered each of those chapters into a document, with page breaks between each chapter. Here are the chapters I eventually ended up with in my life story:

1. And I made an abridgment of the records...(Summary)
2. The hearts of the children shall turn to their fathers...(Genealogy)
3. And it came to pass, I grew in stature and understanding...
4. And it came to pass, that the Elders of the Education System determined I should learn....(Schooling)
5. In the service of the Lord...(Missionary experiences)
6. The Elders of the Education System determined I should go to the University....
7. Ye are my friends
8. And ye shall cleave unto your wife and none else...
9. Multiply and replenish the earth...
10. By the sweat of your brow...
11. As for me and my house, we will serve the Lord...(Church service)
12. And these signs shall follow them that believe...(Spiritual experiences)
13. Significant people in my life

14. Significant personal events
15. Honors
16. Athletics
17. Significant Church events
18. Significant world events
19. Cars / Trucks we've owned
20. Dan on Dan
21. Pictures
22. Talks

Next, I went through each chapter and listed bullet points of the items that would be in that chapter. For example, in the *Significant World Events* chapter, I listed the following events I would later flesh out:

• Kennedy assassinations
• Vietnam War
• Man on the moon
• Nixon resignation
• Challenger explosion
• Berlin wall / collapse of the Soviet Union
• Various presidential tenures
• 9/11
• The Great Recession

And so on. After entering the bullet points under each of the chapter headings, I went back and began the actual writing. Invariably, as I wrote, other events or times in my life would come to mind, so I would just go to the chapter that event fit in and jotted down the bullet point to capture it. Sometimes, the event didn't fit nicely into a chapter, so I just created a new chapter for the event.

After a number of years, my life story was ready for prime time. I had decided I wanted it to be a permanent record, so I sought a self publisher and self published the book. I used Diggypod, but you can find other self publishers by Googling them. I printed enough copies for my children, grandchildren, forecast grandchildren, parents, siblings and my wife and me.

Continue searching for documents in your home that you would consider valuable if you were able to find them for your ancestors. Baptismal or confirmation certificates, diplomas, newspaper articles, obituaries, photographs, military records, divorce decrees, etc. All of these help paint the picture that is you and your family.

Genealogy versus Family History
As you work (play!) in genealogy, you may run into the term *Family History*. Is family history the same as genealogy? Well, I don't know if there is a formal difference, or if there has been differentiating definitions of each, but in my mind, they are two related but different bodies of work. *Genealogy* I see as the facts about our ancestors: names, dates, places, etc., while *family history* I see as much more – the facts beyond the facts: stories about the lives of your ancestors, their hopes and dreams, accomplishments and tragedies. Here's an example about the differences between the two, using information about my second great grandmother:

Genealogy
Name: Lucy Arabella Phillips McCollough
Birth date: 20 June, 1860
Birth Place: Waynesburg, Greene County, Pennsylvania
Married: William Lindsay McCollough, 19 August, 1883 in Waynesburg,
     Greene County, Pennsylvania

Children: Theodora Charity, Birdie Franklin, William Lindsey, Lucy
    Marie, Hazeldean Gertrude
Death date: 18 June, 1948
Death place: Ralston, Pawnee County, Oklahoma

Family History
In addition to the above:

> My second great grandmother, Lucy Arabella Phillips McCollough,
> was called Grandma Mac. In 1892, when her sister became
> pregnant out of wedlock, she and her sister left town to go "visit
> family." They returned about a year later, claiming her sister's two-
> month-old child was hers, and she reared him as her own. She was
> well regarded in the community and the family, and was consid-
> ered to be a kind and gentle person. She loved animals and always
> had at least one dog. She loved her great grandson – my father – and
> he loved to go visit his Grandma Mac.
>
> In a bit of bizarre irony, a falling tree killed her father, and a falling
> radio pole killed her husband. After her husband's death, she
> continued to run the ranch by herself.

I often have the opportunity to speak about genealogy to church groups and
genealogy societies, opportunities I truly enjoy. Not long before I wrote this
book, I spoke to a women's group at my church. Seems a number of the
women were feeling stressed about not being able to spend time doing
genealogy. I helped them understand their definition was too narrow. If
they focused on family history instead of merely genealogy, they could do
family history easily. Telling their children stories about their grandparents
(her parents) and great grandparents is a way of forging the connection
between generations. Doing photo-histories of your family (aka: *scrapbooking*)

qualifies as family history work. Be sure to add the names and ages of the people in your photos, along with the date and place the photo was taken and *voila!* – instant genealogy / family history!

I have begun interviewing my aging parents, recording their memories of their ancestors – their parents, grandparents, great grandparents. I ask about stories that help illustrate their personalities, likes, dislikes, dreams, etc. It has been fun for me to learn more about these ancestors of mine, and I think my parents have enjoyed spending time reminiscing about these people, some of them now gone for many decades.

4. MASTERING LIBRARY RECORDS

A library is not a luxury but one of the necessities of life.
– Henry Ward Beecher

I would agree with the good reverend Beecher above – a library is one of the necessities of life. And my sentiment relates not only to my personal life (I am somewhat of a bibliophile), but also in the world of genealogy.

Now – for those of you who are computer savvy and think the only way to find a record is on the Internet, don't turn up your noses just yet. It is true that many records are finding their way online these days – a happening that is truly to be celebrated by genealogists. But there are also many records that are not online, nor will they be for a number of years, if ever. And that's where libraries come in.

Libraries in and of themselves are enticing to me. Add the prefix *Genealogy* to *Library* and it is all I can do to stay away, and once there, all I can do to tear myself away when it is time to leave. An example here may suffice:

Many years ago, in the late 1980s, I had a business trip to Richmond, Virginia. I knew from previous research that my ancestors lived for nearly 200 years in the southwestern corner of Virginia, living and dying, loving and fighting there. I also knew that many of the state's genealogy records had been gathered to the state genealogy library in Richmond. I planned to stay a few days after my business trip and do what genealogy I could.

My business trip ended on Wednesday evening. As the library opened the next morning, I was there, pencil and tablet in hand. Almost immediately I ran across my ancestors – hundreds of them, perhaps thousands. They were in census records, vital records: birth, death, marriage records.

Alas, at that time, the Virginia state genealogy library did not have machines that would copy microfilm, so I had to transcribe by hand all the records of my ancestors. I worked until closing time on Thursday evening. I returned first thing on Friday morning and searched and wrote and wrote until they were turning out the lights and trying to get me to stop. I returned the next day – Saturday – and worked until the library closed at noon. I must have spent every minute of 24 or 25 hours (ten hours on the weekdays and half a day Saturday) writing furiously. I didn't stop for restroom breaks, lunch or dinner – I just wrote continuously for two and a half days.

I had remarkable experiences with my Quillen ancestors – in my "mind's eye" I saw them born, saw siblings born and die, parents die, saw them marry, lose children and spouse, and then be laid to rest themselves. It was a sweet time, a sacred time, as I followed these forebears of mine from cradle to grave.

GENEALOGY LIBRARIES OF THE LDS CHURCH
Family History Library
One of the pre-eminent libraries in "genealogydom" is the Family History Library (FHL) in Salt Lake City, Utah. For about 175 years, members of the Church of Jesus Christ of Latter-day Saints – the Mormons – have been busy gathering the names of their ancestors for religious reasons. They believe families can live together in heaven forever, and they seek the names of their ancestors to create linkages between themselves and their ancestors.

This work by the Latter-day Saints has benefitted genealogists all over the world. Not only have they been busy gathering genealogical information for nearly two centuries, but they make it available to genealogists, whether members of their church or not.

Their main genealogy library is located at 35 North West Temple Street in Salt Lake City (tel. 866-406-1830). It is open Monday from 7:30am to 5:00pm, and Tuesday through Saturday from 7:30am to 10:00pm. It is closed on Sundays, January 1, July 4, Thanksgiving and December 24 and 25. There is no charge for admission to the FHL. Here's a sampling of what you will find if you are ever fortunate enough to visit the FHL:

- 142,000 square feet of genealogical delight
- 2.4 million rolls of microfilmed records
- 727,000 microfiche pages of records
- 356,000 books of genealogical records
- 100 part- and full-time professional research consultants
- 700 volunteer staff members trained to assist genealogists

The LDS Church estimates that over three *billion* names of deceased people are included in their holdings. And it's all available to you. If you are able to visit, you will undoubtedly feel like a kid in a candy store. If you find yourself overwhelmed by what you find there, you might consider taking their ten-minute orientation tour. Genealogical records are available at the FHL from the United States, Canada, Europe, the British Isles, Latin America, Asia and Africa. The vast majority of the collection contains information on individuals that died prior to 1930.

Legions of volunteers go throughout the world, filming the world's genea- logical records. Those digitized images find their way back to the FHL and are made available to genealogists. Records have been filmed in over one hundred and ten countries, territories and possessions, and over two hundred cameras are currently active filming genealogy records in forty-five countries at this time.

I was once fortunate enough to work just eight blocks from the FHL for a few years. For awhile, I got in the habit of taking my morning break at 11:45am, lunch at noon, and my afternoon break at 1:00pm, giving me ninety minutes to do genealogical research. While this looked like a great plan on paper, it didn't pan out. I found myself constantly taking a half-day's vacation to remain in the library and continue following some thread of a clue I had found! While my ancestors loved that, my wife did not.

Family History Centers
If time, distance or expense prohibit you from visiting the FHL in Salt Lake City, don't despair. There are several options available to assist you. The first we'll discuss are Family History Centers.

Think of Family History Centers (FHCs) as branch offices of the FHL in Salt Lake City. The LDS Church maintains over 4,500 of these branch offices in eighty countries throughout the world. In fact, you probably have one in your neighborhood and don't even know it. Most FHCs are located in local meetinghouses of the LDS Church. They are staffed by volunteers, so the hours are somewhat irregular – you'll have to check with the local meetinghouse to see what days and times your local FHC is open.

What will you find if you visit an FHC? Well, you won't find records containing three billion names, as you would if you visited FHL. But many of those records are available to you through a lending system that is as efficient as any in the world. Once you identify a microfilm or book you would like, you identify it to the volunteer who is working at the FHC the day you are there. For a small fee ($5.50 per microfilm roll), they will order the source you are seeking. Delivery varies, but is usually one week. Once the item arrives, it will remain in the library for you to view for six weeks. This is a very popular program – each month, over 100,000 microfilm rolls are sent to FHCs around the world – over a million rolls per year!

Most FHCs in the United States have subscriptions to Ancestry.com for their patrons to use – a nice perq if you do not have an Ancestry.com subscription yourself. And although it is a free service, you can also access FamilySearch.org at the FHCs.

Perhaps the best assets at the FHCs are the volunteers who freely give their time and talents to assist individuals in their area to use the FHC to its greatest purpose. They delight in helping people find their ancestors, and move further up their family tree.

You can find the FHC nearest to you by going to *www.familysearch.org/locations*.

State Genealogy Libraries

Earlier in this book I mentioned the Virginia State Library, in which I had such a phenomenal genealogy research experience with my Virginia ancestors. You too can have such an experience, as all states

> **Family History Centers are like branch libraries of the LDS Church's Family History Library.**

have a State Library and/or Archives location. I have provided a list of the state libraries of our nation in **Appendix A.**

Earlier I mentioned my genealogy adventure at the Virginia State Library in Richmond. Following are some of the collections available to genealogists at the library:

- Manuscript sources
- Tax records
- Military records
    Colonial militia
    French & Indian War
    Revolutionary War
    Civil War (a particularly important collection, since part of the state's men fought for the South and part fought for the North)
    War of 1812
    World War I
    Other wars
- Bounty Land Warrants
    Land office records
- Vital statistics
    Birth
    Marriage
    Death
    Church registers
    Bible records
- County records
    Deeds
    Wills
    Divorce
    Marriage bonds
- Census records
    Federal records
    State records
    Mortality schedules
- Private papers, Bible records, state records

I used to work in downtown Denver, just a handful of blocks from the State Archives and the State Library. For a time, I was a volunteer for Random Acts of Genealogical Kindness (*www.raogk.org*), a tremendous genealogy organization. I fielded numerous requests to look up various kinds of records at the state archives or the state library. Through those efforts I became aware of the various collections both locations held, and was able to help a few genealogists who couldn't just drop in for a visit over their lunch hour to peruse their holdings.

The Colorado State Library has a number of collections, and they are similar to many other state libraries across the US. Their records include:

- Over 160 newspaper collections (some indexed, some not) from 1859 to present
- Indexed obituary collections
- Indexed birth notices
- Indexed marriage notices
- Colorado pioneer records
- Colorado vital records
- Biographies
- Naturalization records
- State census records
- Federal census records
- Rosters of Colorado military men
- Hispanic genealogy records
- African American genealogy records
- Cemetery records
- Mortuary records
- Street directories

This is just a sampling of their holdings, and they aren't all that different

Find out where the state library in my ancestors' state is; visit it and get lots of genealogy data.

from other state libraries around the nation. It's definitely worth your while to stop by and check out what your state genealogy library has to offer.

Note: you might be asking yourself: "What's so special about street directories? Why did Quillen mention they are in the Colorado State Library collection? Seems rather odd." Good question – glad you asked! One of the difficulties of finding our ancestors is, well, finding them! If you are like me, you have ancestors that just up and disappear from one place, and show up years later someplace else. If you only use federal censuses to track them, that's a ten-year gap, and a lot can happen in ten years (look at your own life!). Not to mention the gap between the 1880 census and the 1900 census since the majority of the 1890 census was lost in a fire – that's a twenty-year gap.

Sometimes you can bridge that gap a bit by using state censuses, but those were typically every five years, so you can still have a sizeable gap. Street directories help you discern when an ancestor left an area (he was in the 1872 street directory and not the 1873 street directory for a particular locale) and/ or when he arrived in a new area (he wasn't in the 1872 street directory, but was in the 1873 directory). If from other records you know he had children born in the 1870s, you can with some certainty identify their place of birth. It is in the area you find their father residing that you'll want to check for birth certificates for the children, and perhaps even marriage records, depending on the situation.

Using the same logic, you can perhaps narrow a time and place of death for an ancestor – he was alive at the time of the printing of the street directory, but the next year's directory did not list him.

Genealogy Society Libraries

One of my favorite genealogy libraries is the genealogy library run by the Schuyler County (Illinois) Genealogy Society. Efforts of their members to preserve and share the genealogical stories of Schuyler County's people are inspiring! As I have searched and researched, I have found that as wonderful as they are, they are in good company: genealogy societies across the nation man (woman?) genealogy libraries so that genealogists can find their long-lost ancestors.

Sometimes the genealogy society libraries are housed in their own building, sometimes on the floor or section of a larger building – perhaps the county or town library.

I'll use as an example the society I mentioned before from Schuyler County, Illinois. The *Schuyler County Historical Society* (*www.schuylerhistory.org*) resides in the former court house / jail in the booming metropolis of Rushville, Illinois. Following are a few of the genealogy collections they have:

- Family history files
- Family event files
- Vital records: birth, marriage, death
- Historic newspapers
- Cemetery records
- Old journals
- Civil War muster records

Like many genealogy societies, the Schuyler County Historical Society is a non-profit organization. Generally you can join such societies for a reasonable fee — $25 or thereabouts seems to be the going rate. For your membership, you'll often receive newsletters about current collections, new collections, collections undergoing indexing, etc. The Schuyler County Historical Society produces a quarterly publication called *The Schuylerite*, which is chock full of genealogical information in each edition. Information contains things like abstracts of vital statistics records (birth, marriage, and death records), obituaries from a certain time period, abstracts from wills, excerpts from the Schuyler County history, etc. A great section is the *Queries* section, where members of the society post queries about family information they are looking for.

Many genealogy societies, including the Schuyler County Historical Society, provide research services for genealogists who can't visit their library personally. Schuyler County has to be at the lower end of the fee spectrum, as they charge only $10 an hour to search their collections for information.

Some genealogy societies focus on geographic areas – town, county or state, even regions: the New England Historic Genealogical Society, for example. Others focus on ethnic research: Afro-American Historical and Genealogical Society, Hispanic Genealogical Society, Swedish Genealogical Society of Minnesota, etc. Some even focus on surnames: The Hudson Family Association, Throckmorton Family Genealogical Forum, etc.

In fact, several years ago, quite by accident, I ran across the Hudson Family Association. I jotted their contact information down, then sent them $75, indicating I hoped it would cover the cost of membership to their society, as well as have a little left over to be able to get some past copies of any newsletters they published.

I am by nature an optimist, so I was cautiously optimistic that the Hudson Family Association would be able to assist me in my Hudson ancestral pursuit. I was totally unprepared for the amount and quality of assistance they gave me.

Within days I received a note welcoming me to the Hudson Family Association. They explained that the association was formed to further genealogical research on the family line, and asked whether I would be willing to share information about my side of the family. I fired off a letter with what little I knew about my Hudson family heritage. My grandmother was a Hudson, and I knew little beyond her father. But I sent off what I had, something along these lines:

> I am William Daniel Quillen, married to Bonita Blau Quillen. My parents are William Edgar and Versie Lee Lowrance Quillen. My mother's parents are Elzie Lee Lowrance and Alma Hudson. Alma Hudson's parents were Francis Marion Hudson and Margaret Ellen Turpin. I am told that Francis Marion Hudson was named after some ancestors

A few weeks later, I received my first copy of the bulletin *Hudsoniana*, the Hudson Family Association newsletter. One section was devoted to welcoming new members. Imagine my unbounded joy when I found the following entry:

> **Welcome New Members!**
> Quillen, W. Daniel:
> William Daniel QUILLEN, born _____, Lynwood, Los Angeles, CA married _____ Bonita BLAU; children: William Michael, Katie Scarlet, Joseph Daniel, Andrew Teague, Emily, Jesse Lee Blaine.
> Versie Lee LOWRANCE, born McClain, OK, married 13 July 1951 William Edgar QUILLEN, born Norman, OK;
> Alma HUDSON, born 24 Apr 1913, Stephens, OK, married 5 Oct 1932 Elzie Lee LOWRANCE, born 24 Feb 1906, Wayne, OK;

Francis Marion HUDSON, born 13 Nov 1877, Pope, AR, died 12 Jan 1960, Los Angeles, CA, married 1909 Margaret Ellen TURPIN;

Jeremiah HUDSON, born 1851, AR, died 1914, Dibble, OK, married about 1873 Frances DUVALL, AR;

Francis Marion HUDSON, born 20 March 1829, Lauderdale County, AL, married about 1848 Mary ____;

Jeremiah HUDSON, living 1830 in Lauderdale County, AL, married Lavina JONES, living in 1830 in Lauderdale County, AL;

Levi HUDSON, married Hannah ___;

Major HUDSON, born about 1690, died 16 Nov. 1781, Worchester County, MD, married Martha GILLETT;

Henry HUDSON, born 8 July 1669, Somerset County, Maryland, died 24 Dec 1720, Somerset County, MD married (1) ____ LUDLONG?, (2) Ellis DENNIS;

Henry HUDSON, born about 1642, Accomack County, Virginia, died about 1710, Somerset County, Maryland, married about 1664 Lydia SMITH;

Richard HUDSON, born 1605, England, died about 1657, Northampton County, Virginia, married (1) Mary ____, married (2) Mrs. Mary HAYES, married (3) Barbara JACOBS;

William HUDSON, born about 1570, London, England, married about 1603 Alice Turner;

Henry HUDSON born about 1541

They had taken the scant information I had provided them and tied me back in a direct line of ancestors to 1541 – 12 generations and 450 years! A subsequent request from me provided family group sheets on every family member along with documentation and source citations for most of the names and dates – hundreds of names and a great deal of vital statistic information. A wonderful find indeed.

A genealogy society library that may not leap immediately to mind is the Daughters of the American Revolution Genealogical Society Library (*www.dar.org/library/library*). Here is a bit about them from their website (I **highlighted** in bold the section specific to their genealogical work):

> Does *my* family have a genealogy society already working on my family's genealogy?

The DAR, founded in 1890 and headquartered in Washington, D.C., is a non-profit, non-political volunteer women's service organization dedicated to promoting patriotism, preserving American history, and securing America's future through better education for children.

DAR members volunteer more than 250,000 hours annually to veteran patients, award thousands of dollars in scholarships and financial aid each year to students, and support schools for underserved children with annual donations exceeding one million dollars.

As one of the most inclusive genealogical societies in the country, DAR boasts 170,000 members in 3,000 chapters across the United States and internationally. Any woman 18 years or older — regardless of race, religion, or ethnic background — who can prove lineal descent from a patriot of the American Revolution, is eligible for membership.

Encompassing an entire downtown city block, DAR National Headquarters houses **one of the nation's premier genealogical libraries**, one of the foremost collections of pre-industrial Ameri can decorative arts, Washington's largest concert hall, and an extensive collection of early American manuscripts and imprints.

A visit to their website to look around is impressive, and once you hit the DAR Library tab, you'll have a wonderful time checking out their various genealogy collections. Here are a few:

• Biographies
• Histories
• Genealogies / pedigrees
• Manuscripts
• Vital statistics (birth, marriage, death)
• Abstracts

Just poking around their electronic library card catalog, I found:

• 287 titles covering vital statistics, including
    New Hampshire index to births to 1900
    New Hampshire index to marriages to 1900
    Allen county, Kentucky statistics revisited 1852—1904: births, deaths, marriages
• Over 1,000 titles about wills, including items like:
    Kentucky early court records: abstracts of early wills, deeds and marriages
    A genealogical collection of South Carolina wills and records
    Anderson County Wills, 1830-1913
• Over 1,000 titles about cemeteries, including items like:
    Athens County, Ohio cemetery inscriptions
    Massachusetts Cemetery records
    Avon township cemetery inscriptions, Lake County, Illinois

When searching for genealogy societies in your area, or the areas where your ancestors lived, the Internet is a powerful ally. If you can't find a society by Googling *(Name of county or state) Genealogy Society*, also try searching for *(Name of county or state) Historical Society*. That may yield the information you are seeking. And remember to search for groups that focus on a particular surname.

Plain Old Libraries

In your rush to ferret out genealogy libraries and state libraries, don't forget plain old neighborhood libraries. This is particularly true in the areas where your ancestors came from! If you are like me, you live a long ways

The DAR might have some great records about my ancestors!

from the places your ancestors lived. My ancestors lived in Pennsylvania, Illinois, Missouri, Oklahoma, New Jersey, Virginia and Ireland. Small town or county libraries in the areas where your ancestors lived may well have information about your ancestors that are found nowhere else! Perhaps a *Town History* has been published about the founders of the town or the early pioneers of the area. Perhaps one or more of your relatives served on a school board, a draft board, a city or town council and a biography was penned for him or her. Maybe you'll find missing information on an elusive ancestor in a County history or in newspaper archives kept in the local library.

Years ago, I was fortunate to find a county history that contained quite a bit of information on my fourth great grandfather, who lived out in the country near Rushville, Schuyler County, Illinois. It was written in a book called *Old Settlers of Schuyler County, Illinois,* located in the Rushville Library and Schuyler County Historical Society building.

This paragraph, in an excerpt from the township history section of the above-mentioned book, names two of my fourth great grandfathers, Samuel Horney and Drury Sellers:

> By this time Littleton Township was well known among the settlements of the county, and the rush of immigration makes it difficult to follow the settlements in their natural order. But among the settlers who came to the township in those early days, and made it their permanent place of abode, we may mention the following: Randolph Rose, **Drury Sellers**, Michael Matheney, Joseph Logan, **Col. Samuel Horney**, George Garrison, William Lambert, James DeWitt, John S. Walker, Samuel Dodds, Joseph W. Snyder, Adam Walker, John Seward and D. C. Payne.

My third great grandfather, Leonidas Horney, was identified several paragraphs later as the County Surveyor. Other references to Samuel Horney included:

> This early settlement was augmented in March, 1825, by the arrival of two brothers, Samuel and Manlove Horney, with families, consisting of a wife and one child. These pioneers were natives of North Carolina, but came from St. Clair County, Illinois, where they had been living since 1818. They settled in Buena Vista, Samuel, on the S. W. ° of section 14, and Manlove, on an adjoining quarter. They both resided here until 1834, when they moved up into Littleton.

The genealogical information in that last paragraph is evident: telling me when Samuel Horney and his brother arrived in Littleton Township, Schuyler County, Illinois, that both came with a wife and child, were from North Carolina and lived in St. Clair County, Illinois between 1818 and

March 1825. Later in the book, extensive biographies of my third and fourth great grandfathers Horney were provided. The genealogy for my fourth great grandfather, Samuel Horney, included the following genealogically relevant data:

- His name
- His father and mother's names, their birth places and dates
- His mother's death date
- His step-mother's name, birth date and place, and marriage date to his father
- The number of siblings and half siblings Samuel had
- Samuel's birth place and date
- Where Samuel's father lived and what dates he moved, and where (helpful when trying to determine birth places of children)
- The death dates and places of Samuel's father and step-mother
- The name of Samuel's wife, and her birth date and place
- Samuel's enlistment in the War of 1812, his rank and service
- The name of Samuel's wife's parents
- The name of Samuel's only child, and his birth date and place
- The regiment and company Samuel served in during the Blackhawk War

In addition, there was information about his standing in the community ("…highly beloved and respected by his fellow citizens…"), roles he had played in the founding of the county, jobs and political offices he held (Justice of the Peace, which he held for 30 years), and his political views ("He is a supporter of the old Jeffersonian principles.")

National Archives

I have saved the largest libraries for last! Though not libraries, per se, I have chosen to include the nation's archives in this section of the book. I

County histories = worth looking for!

have visited several of our national archives, and they are all very impressive, not to mention incredibly useful resources for researchers.

There are a number of locations of the National Archives geographically dispersed around the United States. Each contains a valuable cache of genealogical information, including all the US Censuses that are available for the public to view. There are fourteen main National Archives locations, but there are other non-principal archival facilities spread throughout the nation. These latter sites include Presidential Libraries, microfilm locations, textual research locations, military records locations, Library of Congress, etc. You can find a complete listing at *www.archives.gov/locations*. I have included a listing of the main National Archives locations in **Appendix B** at the end of the book.

The National Archives are accessible to genealogists either online, through microfilm, or through personal visits. The website for NARA (National Archives and Records Administration) is *www.archives.gov*. The National Archives are the repository of many records that are of particular interest to genealogists. Below is an example of the collections available at the archives:

• Military records
• Immigration records
• Naturalization records
• Passport applications
• Wills and probate records
• Land records
• And many more....

As a genealogist, I am particularly enamored with US military records, as some of my earliest and most significant genealogical successes came through such records. (In fact, I was so thrilled with them, I wrote a book to help others have the same kind of success I had: *Mastering Census and Military Records*, another in the *Essentials* series of genealogy books).

I'd love to tell you all these wonderful records were online, available and accessible by the click of your mouse. Alas, such is not the case, although progress is being made in digitizing their holdings. To accomplish this digitization, the National Archives has forged partnerships with for-profit organizations like Ancestry.com and Fold3.com, and more and more of their records collections are coming online.

Notwithstanding those partnerships, the vast majority of their records are available only by snail mail or visits to National Archives facilities. To request records via mail, you must fill out a request, mail it, wait up to two months for a response, etc. (In lightning fast response to new technology, you can now send a query about the status of your request via e-mail after your request has been in for ten days!) The cost for a successful search is $25. When you complete the form requesting the information, you'll be given the option of paying by credit card, or they will invoice you for the successful search. There is no charge if their search is unsuccessful.

If you want to check military records out yourself, military records for the 20th century are kept at:

National Personnel Records Center
Military Personnel Records (NPRC-MPR)
9700 Page Avenue
St. Louis, MO 63132-5100

They contain the military personnel, health and medical records of discharged and deceased military veterans from all branches of the armed forces (more on this later).

Records of military personnel prior to 1912 (World War I) are located in Washington DC at:

National Archives
700 Pennsylvania Avenue
Washington, DC 20408-0001

Following are the records held at that National Archives location:

• Volunteer military service (1775 to 1902)
• US Army military records (1789 to 1917) (Officers prior to June 30, 1917, enlisted men prior to October 31, 1912)
• US Navy records (1798 to 1902)
• US Marine Corps (1789 to 1904)
• US Coast Guard and its predecessors (1791 to 1919)
• Civil War Service and pension records (Union as well as Confederate)

Whether you view military records online of visit one of the National Archives locations, you'll want to have an idea of what kinds of records are available. Here are some of the types of military records available:

• **Bounty Land Warrants** – payment for service in several of the early wars in our nation's history (1776 to 1855). Veterans received grants of public lands for their service.
• **Enlistment Records** – while not a lot of genealogical information is usually found in enlistment records, you can find out what your ancestor looked like: height, weight, hair and eye color, complexion, size of hands and feet, etc., as well as marital status.
• **Record of Events** – not much genealogical value here, as they mostly just provide information about troop movements. It will tell you what battles your ancestor fought in.

VISITING & RESEARCHING AT THE NATIONAL ARCHIVES

When you visit a National Archives facility to do research, it's not exactly like strolling into your local library to do a research project. There are special rules you'll need to follow; here are a few:

• Upon arrival your first time, be prepared to watch a short presentation (15 minutes or so) on researching at the National Archives.
• To view original documents, you must register to obtain a Research Identification Card. Bring a photo ID and be able to describe your research project. It must be a project that can be reasonably pursued at NARA.
• Lockers are provided for personal belongings, including purses, briefcases, etc. Light jackets or sweaters may be worn in the research rooms, but if you remove them, you may be asked to put them in your locker. Lockers cost a quarter, but the quarter is returned when you retrieve your items.
• You are not allowed to bring notebooks, personal notes, etc. into the research rooms. You may bring a laptop computer in, and possibly a digital camera (but you must get permission for the latter first). Note: Some research rooms have few electrical outlets.
• Self-service and staff photocopying is allowed, depending on the section and the items to be copied. Self-serve copies are $.25 each.
• You may not use ink pens in your note taking. Either bring a pencil, or one will be provided for you. Do not bother bringing your own paper, notebooks, journals, etc. NARA will provide paper and note cards for you.
• As of this writing (but check before you go!), hours of public operation are Monday, Tuesday and Saturday, 9:00am to 5:00pm, Wednesday through Friday, 9:00am to 9:00pm.
• Pull times (where staff will go and pull your requests from the archives) are 10:00am, 11:00am, 1:30pm and 2:30pm, with an extra pull time of 3:30pm Wednesday through Friday. No records are pulled from the stacks on Saturdays or evenings.

These rules and regulations may sound a little over the top, but they are necessary to preserve these precious documents so they will continue to be available to researchers for generations to come. Rather than be annoyed (or amused), appreciate the effort – after all, these requirements have ensured that these original documents have been preserved so that you can view them!

- **Compiled Military Service Records** (CMSR) – Each soldier has a CMSR for every regiment in which he served. Muster rolls, requests for leave, injuries and death were reported on CMSRs.
- **Draft registration card (World War I)** – 98% of the men between the ages of 18 and 45 completed draft registration cards during World War I, and they provide information about birth date and place and they often identify a man's spouse or parent's name.
- **Draft registration card (World War II)** – men born between 28 April 1877 and 16 February 1897 were asked to register so the government could get a handle on the size of the work force if all its younger men went to war. Like their World War I cousins, these registration cards provide birth date and place and identify a man's spouse or parents.
- **Pension Records** – probably the most valuable of the military records from a genealogical standpoint. You may well find out a great deal of information about your veteran ancestor, including his:
  - birth date and place
  - marriage date and place
  - death date and place
  - wife's maiden name, marriage date and place

Note: Confederate soldiers' pension applications were made to the state from which they served, not the federal government. Those records are held at the state level.)

Before we leave pensions, I have to share a great experience I had with a pension application. As I mentioned at the outset of this book, I like to use my family members whenever possible to illustrate search techniques and tactics. When I was writing the previously mentioned *Mastering Census and Military Records*, I wanted to use one of my ancestors who had a pension application from the Revolutionary War. Alas, no name came to mind, so I just sort of pulled a name out of a hat. I decided John was a pretty common name in the 18th century, so searched for a revolutionary War pension application for John Quillen. None appeared, but there was one for John Quillin. Since that is a common misspelling / alternate spelling for my name, I decided to use it in the book. Here is a transcription of that pension (I have **highlighted** the **genealogical data** that exists):

> **State of North Carolina**
> **Stokes County**
> On this **24**[th] **day of August, 1833**, personally appeared unto me…John Quillin, **aged seventy-six years**, who being first sworn according to law **at his own place of residence** in the afore-mentioned county, doth on his Oath make the following declaration in order to obtain the benefit of the Act of Congress passed 7th June 1832. First he states that from the infirmities of old age together with the fact that at certain times the loss of his memory makes it impossible for him to remember the precise dates of his service as a soldier of the Revolution, but as well as he can recollect, he entered the service of the United States under the following named officers who served as hereinafter stated. That he first entered the service as a drafted private in Surry County, North Carolina in Captain Henry Smith's company of militia infantry…. (following this were officers' names and descriptions of campaigns John was on)….Near the Savannah River, the applicant states that he hired a certain William Fields as a substitute to serve the balance of his tour in order that he might **return home to his wife who was in a delicate situation** at the time…
> Of the seven interrogatories prescribed by the War Department, he answers them as follows (to wit):
> 1st – that **he was born in Cumberland County, North Carolina**
> 2nd – that he has no record of his age, only traditionary that **he was born in March 1757**

3rd – that he lived **in Surry County North Carolina when called into the service**….

4th – answer as above

5th – that from his being subject to fitts and consequent loss of his recollection, he cannot name all the officers any more than he has named already or Regiments

6th – that he does not remember of receiving a written discharge, and if he did, he has lost it

7th – he has no one present, but has a number of individuals that will testify as to his character as to veracity and belief of his services as a soldier of the Revolution, there being no clergyman for a considerable distance from him renders it very inconvenient for one's certificate.

There were ten pages in the pension application, including the cover of the envelope all the papers were in, as well as seven other pages, including statements from several neighbors and a man who averred that he served with John during parts of his service. Let's check out the genealogical information available from this pension application:

1. **State of North Carolina, Stokes County** – identifies where John was on a certain date;

2. **24 August, 1833** – the certain date John was at Stokes County, NC;

3. **…at his own place of residence…** — The statement was taken at his residence on the above date in the above-stated county and state;

4. **aged seventy-six** — he was seventy-six (76) years old on 24 August 1833;

5. **return home to his wife** — He was married;

6. **his wife who was in a delicate situation** – this was often a euphemism for pregnancy (but could also have meant she was very ill);

7. **born in Cumberland County, North Carolina** – John's birth place;

8. **he was born in March 1757** – John's
    birth month and date, according to
    traditionary….

As you can see, this 250-year-old document has a cache of wonderful genealogical tidbits about this gentleman, a patri-
otic (and failing-memoried) soldier of the Revolution!

> **Military records
> may provide
> significant genea-
> logical information.**

Just prior to sending *Mastering Census & Military Records* to my publisher,
I discovered that my fifth great grandfather was John Quillin, born March
1757 in Cumberland County, North Carolina – this very man!

Here's an overview of some of the other records collections available at the
National Archives:

• **Immigration records**

Passenger lists – you may be surprised to learn that immigrants to
America arrived in more ports than Ellis Island! Passenger lists often
provide information that identify your immigrant ancestor's roots, as
well as the next generation that was left behind in their home country.

Censuses – a number of state and federal censuses asked for
birthplaces, year of immigration, whether or not your ancestor was
naturalized and if so, the year of their naturalization.

Emigration records – these were kept in the country of your
ancestors' departure and often provide important information.

Certificates of Arrival – these short documents provide your
ancestor's name, date and port of arrival and ship they arrived on. While
not providing much in the way of genealogical value, it gives you a date
certain when your ancestor arrived, and may lead to other genealogy-
laden documents.

• **Naturalization records**

Declarations of Intention – These are documents completed by immigrants, often upon arrival in America, indicating their desire and intent to immigrate permanently. They are some of the best genealogy-related documents you find for your immigrating ancestors. Depending on when they arrived, great gobs of genealogical information are often provided, including birth dates and places of your immigrant ancestor, his wife and children.

Petitions for Naturalization – like their younger brother (Declarations of Intention), Petitions for Citizenship provide a significant amount of genealogical data including birth dates and places of the immigrant and his family.

Oaths of Allegiance – every immigrant requesting US citizenship was required to take and sign an Oath of Allegiance. There isn't much information of genealogical value, but oaths of allegiance may lead you to other information-laden documents. They also provide you with a time and place for your ancestor, which is valuable when searching for genealogical information.

• **Passport applications**

Immigrants often left family in the old country, and frequently visited them. Passport applications often included birth date and place information for the traveler as well as the people he was visiting.

Immigrants often left businesses that needed attending to, farms that needed to be sold, and family members whose estates needed to be cared for. Passports provide valuable information about immigrants at the time of their visits to their home country.

Passport applications may include information about the naturalization status of the immigrant, and may even provide the date of naturalization and the court where the naturalization was filed, which will help you find his naturalization papers.

The National Archives contains over two million passports for Americans traveling between 1810 and 1925.

• Wills and probate records

Wills and probate records often identify family members that were unknown from other records. Sons-in-law are named, children, even nieces and nephews.

Wills were often witnessed by immediate as well as extended family members.

• Land records

Land records may seem like an odd place to seek genealogical data. But they provide you with proof that an ancestor lived in a certain place at a certain time, making it possible to focus your search for other more genealogically related documents.

Land was often granted by military service through Bounty Land Warrants. This may lead you to records that provide data about your ancestors.

Deeds were often exchanged between parents and children. Sometimes specific relationships were provided, other times they serve as clues to research further. Deeds required signatures of witnesses – often those signatories were relatives.

• And many more....

Marriage records – don't over look these

Freedmen's Bureau – dealing with former slaves and their families, often provides insights and information about former slaves. Various records for former slaves are available through this great organization, including land, marriage, birth, education, labor records, etc.

Immigration records for specific groups of immigrants: German, Italian, Irish, Chinese, etc.

Court records

Vital records – birth and death certificates, marriage licenses, wills, etc.

I dive much more deeply into the National Archives and the records held there in two other books: *Troubleshooter's Guide to Do-It-Yourself Genealogy* and *Mastering Immigration & Naturalization Records.*

Check out the National Archives!

Directory of Genealogy Libraries

Before we leave the Libraries section, I just have to mention a marvelous website I ran across recently. It is called the *Directory of Genealogy Libraries,* and it is a tremendous asset if you are searching for genealogy libraries in the United States. The website is *www.gwest.org/gen_libs.htm,* and it provides a wonderful state-by-state list of genealogy libraries, as well as national libraries — like the National Archives, LDS Family History library and the DAR genealogy library I mentioned earlier in this chapter.

The *Directory of Genealogy Libraries* website includes the website and physical address of hundreds of genealogy libraries spread across the United States. It's a great source to poke around on.

Internet

Without overstatement, the Internet could be considered the largest, most accessible Genealogy Library in the world! Don't overlook this terrific repository of genealogical information. You're descended from Throckmortons like I am? Then go to the card catalog (Google or Bing or Yahoo or….) and type *Throckmorton genealogy*, and you'll get nearly 27,000 hits. You're a long-lost Quillen cousin? Type *Quillen genealogy* and you'll get over 67,000 hits. Your ancestor was born in Greene County, Pennsyl vania in the 19th century? Try Googling *Greene County birth records* and you'll have to wade through 222,000 hits!

Even for the most intrepid genealogists, 27,000, 67,000 and 222,000 hits are a little daunting. Yes, it's a great deal of information, but how can you possibly check all 27k / 67k / 222k websites? Fortunately for you and me, Google and other search engines allow *Boolean Operators.* Boolean operators are helpful tools that allow you to narrow your search to a manageable size.

Let's take several of the searches I gave as examples above and see if we can narrow them a bit. Let's look at *Quillen genealogy* – the search that yielded 67,000 hits. If I can narrow the search a bit – focus it, so to speak – I will be able to trim the number of websites I have to look at. For example, if I am really trying to find my great grandfather's birth date and place, I can type *Edgar Estil Quillen birth.* Googling that string of words yields 2,370 hits – far better than 67,000 hits. But – still quite a few. Perhaps I can use a Boolean operator to help me narrow the number of hits even further.

As I scan some of the hits I got when I Googled *Edgar Estil Quillen birth,* I note that sometimes Edgar, Estil and Quillen names all belong to different people – there is a list of people on a website:

Edgar Miller and Rodney *Quillen* lived near *Esti*lleville, Virginia.

The first Boolean operators we'll use are plain old ordinary, run-of-the-mill quotation marks: " " – the vanilla ice cream of punctuation marks. Using them helps me narrow the search a bit. By using the following string: "Edgar Estil Quillen" birth, I tell Google to only return hits with the full name exactly as it appears in the string: Edgar Estil Quillen. Googling that quotationed string yields three hits, and all provide the birth information for Edgar Estil Quillen. I'll use my third great grandfather, Leonidas as another example. If I Google:

- Leonidas Horney, I get 2.8 million hits
- "Leonidas Horney," I get 830 hits

Now, Leonidas was a Civil War hero, and many of the 830 hits have to do with his military career. But while that's very interesting, for the time being that's not what I am looking for. I am looking for information about his marriage to the lovely Jane Crawford. Googling the following:

- Leonidas Horney marry Jane Crawford, I get 923,000 hits
- "Leonidas Horney" marry "Jane Crawford," I get 83 hits, most of which deal only with the marriage of Leonidas Horney and Jane Crawford.

Another of the more useful Boolean operators is the word *and*. When Google sees the word *and*, it ties two or more strings of information together. Let's use Leonidas Horney again. If I Google:

- "Leonidas Horney," I get 830 hits
- "Leonidas Horney" and "died," I get 257 hits, most of which deal with Leondas's death during the Civil War.

I cover Boolean operators extensively in *Mastering Online Genealogy*. The two operators above will answer most of your needs. Other Boolean operators include *or, not* and *with*.

A tip o' the hat to fellow genealogist/ blogger Dick Eastman, who suggested the following source on the Internet to find genealogy materials:

I've purchased three cars there. I have acquired countless books to satiate my bibliophile tastes. I've sold books on there (including several first edition Charles Dickens books). I've bought software, computers, printers, monitors from this great cloud-like behemoth. I even bought several remote controls for my television and cable. I even interviewed for a job there once! What is it? Where have I procured these eclectic items? Why, eBay, of course.

As I was writing this book, I went to eBay and typed in *Genealogy* in the *Search* box. I was greeted with over 60,000 hits! The first item was a stack of genealogy books from New England. Well, actually, while the picture listed a stack of about a dozen or so leather-bound books, what was actually being sold was a CD that contained the pdf contents of every page of over 145 books of New England history and genealogy. Included were a number of genealogies, each listing over 200 years of various New England families. As I scanned the various hits, I noted that the same person /company had put together the same types of information (pdfs on CDs) for a number of other states and countries (Virginia, Kentucky, West Virginia, Maryland, Scotland, England, Ireland, etc.)

Other titles included a ton of specific family genealogies:

• *Directory of Ancestral Heads of New England families – 1620 – 1700*
• *The Bevier Family*
• *Captain John Locke (1627 – 1696)*
• *New Hampshire Rye Descendants*
• *And many others*

Some of these items were books, while others were pdfs of those books. The pdfs tended to run about $5 to $6, plus a few bucks for shipping. (**Hint**: make sure you check the shipping charges before buying something very cheap...sometimes eBay listers charge a pittance for the item they are selling, but charge very high shipping and handling fees. Don't get caught in that.)

I decided perhaps 60,000+ items was too many to scan, so I used the *Search* box to see if I could narrow my search. I started by typing *Quillen genealogy*, and came across 50 entries. I was excited until I saw they were all...my books. That's okay – hopefully they'll be helpful to a genealogist or two out there! But I was looking for some genealogy books about my kin.

eBay might yield an interesting genealogical find!

So I tried Throckmorton genealogy – and got four hits, which ended up being two books on CD. I have one of the actual books that was being listed (*Throckmorton Family History* by Frances Grimes Sitherwood) and it is an incredible 413-page book published in 1929 that provides research for the Throckmorton and related families back to 1630 Salem, Massachusetts. I have used it extensively in researching that family. If I didn't have this book, this would have been a tremendous find!

I tried others of my family surnames (Sellers, Horney, McClure, Hudson, etc.) and was often rewarded with more than one book or CD from which to select. While I am a big fan of old books, especially old genealogy books, CDs of the same books have great advantages, especially since you can usually get them for less than $10, including shipping and handling.

Also included were hundreds of county genealogy records, including biographical sketches of citizens, county histories, vital statistics (birth, death, marriage) records, tax records (helpful if you've lost an ancestor between censuses), Civil War censuses, etc.

Less effective, but it did yield some results, was searching for the same types of items in Craigslist. Search the area where your ancestors lived, and you might glean a nugget or two by searching for county histories, genealogies, family surname, etc. It's not as prolific as eBay, but it did provide me with several hits as I poked around.

5. MASTERING CHURCH RECORDS

Churches have been the source of birth, confirmation, baptism, confirmation, marriage and death records for centuries. The key, of course, is to determine to what church your ancestors belonged. Sometimes that's easy – perhaps your ancestors have been aligned with _____ church for hundreds of years. But what if that's not the case? Where do you look for your ancestors' church records?

Are there any clues among your ancestors' belongings, histories, journals, biographies or autobiographies? Recently I discovered that the old family Bible which belonged to my great grandmother and that has found its way to me was a Catholic Bible. That was a surprise to me – once my ancestors left Ireland in the 1600s, I was unaware of Catholicism being part of my ancestry. It may not be, but the fact my great grandmother owned a Catholic Bible is curious indeed, and certainly bears looking into.

Were your ancestors prone to be buried in a particular church yard or religious-related cemetery generation after generation? One of my lines goes back to Greene County, Pennsylvania. Family records indicate that many members of the family were buried in the ME church cemetery. What is the ME church, you ask? It is the Methodist Episcopalian Church, and according to that great source of information *Wikipedia*, the ME Church was the first expression of Methodism in the United States, and became one of the important elements in the United Methodist Church.

Baptist Church Records

With an estimated 100 million adherents, the Baptist Church is considered the largest Protestant church in the world. As you can imagine, with 100 million followers, if they kept records, that would be a lot of birth, marriage and death records!

The Internet may be your most faithful ally when searching for Baptist church records. A recent search on Google with the string *Baptist church records* yielded millions of hits. Some of the hits included:

• Coffee Creek, Indiana Baptist church records, 1822 – 1895
• Southern Baptist Historical Archive and Library
• North Carolina Baptist Church records
• Tunstall Baptist Church Records
> The members list
> The birth list
> The deaths list
> Tunstall marriages – 1813 – 1837
> Gravestones in St. Michael's Tunstall
> Other Tunstall records

Birth, marriage and baptism records were not part of official Baptist records. More often, those records were kept individually by the minister. Most of the records may be limited to minutes of meetings, rosters of congregants, individuals who served in various responsibilities, etc.

A word about that last note – that many official Baptist records don't contain birth, marriage or death records. If your ancestor was Baptist, don't let that dissuade you from checking the records that are available. If nothing else, it may prove that your ancestors were living in the area of that particular Baptist church at a particular time. As we have discussed earlier in this book, sometimes finding your family between censuses is a huge assist to genealogical researchers. If your great grandparents lived in a particular area and were enumerated on the 1860 census, but the 1870 census only lists the wife, it's possible that the husband died sometime during that ten-year interval between censuses. Even if you cannot find record of the husband's death in the church records, you may be able to find him listed in the minutes of the local congregation as a clerk in 1867. That narrows the years you must search for a death record to between the date in 1867 on which his name appeared, and the enumeration date of the 1870 census, making your search much easier. As an example, an index of all congregation members who were mentioned in church minutes for the Coffee Creek, Indiana Baptist Church in 1822 can be found at: *freepages.genealogy.rootsweb. ancestry.com/~fgww/alphalist.html.*

Notwithstanding the official position of the Baptist church that says birth, death and marriage records are not normally part of official church records, through the years I have found more than my fair share of such information among Baptist records. For example, the following information was included in the minutes of the Coffee Creek, Indiana Baptist Church:

- Brother James Fowler departed this life Dec. the 11ᵗʰ, 1823 in the sixty-first year of his age.
- Brother Henry Deputy departed this life December 1852
- Brother James Hammond departed this life February 1853
- Cythy P. COBB married William J. GRAHAM on 14 Aug 1845 in Jefferson County, Indiana
- And this note was added at the end of one of the entries:
    NOTE: Cythy P. COBB married William J. GRAHAM on 14 Aug 1845 in Jefferson County, Indiana. Autobiography of U. M. McGuire says, "William J. married Miss Cobb and began life in a log house on the hill just west of Paris Crossing. Here a son,

Norman, was born and later his mother died." (See June 1852) A few years afterward William Married Sarah HOLBROOK, who became the mother of Elba and Ella, twin girls, and John E. GRAHAM.

If I had been looking for information about Elba and Ella Graham and their brother John E. Graham, this would have been a great find indeed.

The Coffee Creek Baptist Church records also included a marriage book and obituary listing for the members of the Coffee Creek Baptist Church. I even ran across genealogies of some of the main families of some of those Baptist congregations. To see an example, one such genealogy can be found at *freepages.genealogy.rootsweb.ancestry.com/~fgww/HillGenealogy.pdf.* You'll find an eight-generation typewritten genealogy of the Thomas Hill family. Its earliest ancestor was born in 1680, and it ran to 1926. It appears to be well researched and includes many details of the family. If I was seeking information about my ancestor Thomas Hill, born around 1680 in England, I would be thrilled to find this genealogy.

As you search for Baptist church records, it would be well to narrow your search by checking under the congregation name, if you know or can find it: The Fairfax, Oklahoma Baptist Church, Coffee Creek Baptist Church, etc. Specificity like that will help narrow the search among so many potential hits.

Catholic Records

The Roman Catholic Church, in addition to being a wonderful spiritual inspiration to millions of its members worldwide, is also known as one of the 800-pound gorillas in the genealogical rain forest.

> **Official Baptist church records don't have vital statistics; but many do.**

One of the edicts that came out of the 16th-century Council of Trent (an important Ecumenical Council of the Catholic Church) was direction to Roman Catholic clerics throughout the world to faithfully record the significant life events of their parishioners – birth, marriage, death, baptism and confirmation. In most cases, the priests responded faithfully, and about three centuries before governments began requiring birth, marriage and death records, we can find wonderful genealogical data, thanks to these Catholic clerics.

Often, birth records were not kept, but baptismal records were kept of parishioners. Baptism usually followed very closely after birth, but that was not always the case. Baptismal certificates usually included the person's name, birth date, parents and godparents. Sometimes they included the address of the parents, as well as the father's occupation.

For Catholics, baptism and marriage are two of the seven sacraments, and are sacred to them. Because of the Council of Trent, and because of the sacred nature of these two sacraments, meticulous records of these events (along with deaths and confirmations) have been kept for centuries.

Okay – so the Catholic Church kept great records. How, you may ask, do you get access to them? First, collect all the information about the individual whose records you are seeking. His or her name, names of parents, approximate date of the event (birth, marriage, death), and where it occurred.

Once you have gathered that information, it is time to contact the Catholic Church in the area where the event occurred. If it is the only Catholic Church in the area, it may be easy to locate. If not, you may need to contact several parishes (congregations) before locating the correct church. If you don't know the specific parish where your ancestor lived, then you should start at the diocese. Depending on how long ago the event occurred, the records may be kept at the parish level in paper form, or at the diocese level in microfilm or even digital format.

Most dioceses have an archivist or records caretaker. Provide all the information you have about the ancestor whose records you are seeking. Depending on the rules at the particular diocese you are at, the archivist may locate the baptismal / death / marriage record for you, or may refer you to the parish where the records are held. Some parishes have hundreds of years of records, others retain very few on-site. Some churches have halls of records, or records libraries, where you will be expected to search yourself. If that is the case, the archivist will assist you in getting started.

If you want to make a copy of the baptismal, death or marriage certificate, ask for permission to do so. The original certificates are generally kept at the local parish where the event occurred.

One source I read suggested you have a digital camera on hand when you visit, in case you are not allowed to photocopy the original documents.

Many parishes and dioceses have their own websites, and often you'll find information on how to obtain copies of records held at the parish and diocese level. They may also inform you of any restrictions on accessing sacramental records. For example, the website for the Archdiocese of Denver (*http://www.archden.org/index.cfm/ID/68/Searching-for-Records/*) lists the following restrictions on records requests:

1. Records newer than 1930 may only be requested by the individual for whom the event occurred.
2. Records older than 1930 can be obtained by genealogists.
3. The diocese reminds you that access to their files is a *privilege*, not a *right*,

and therefore they encourage you to make an appointment with the archivist to see records.

4. Genealogists need to complete an *Application for Use of Archives* form before access will be allowed. The document is very simple. You complete your name and address, and the reason you are seeking access to the archives. It reminds you that it is a privilege and not a right to access their documents. It informs you that you can access birth and marriage records only for those records that are 85 years old or older. Death records can be accessed prior to 85 years.

5. Genealogists who cannot personally do the research may complete a *Genealogical Request* form. The form tells you that the archivist will do a complimentary half-hour search of the records for you, but if it takes longer than that, the charge is $20 an hour. The form allows you to list the names, parish, event and year of the event for which you are searching.

I checked several other diocese websites, and some were about as specific / restrictive, and others were not nearly so. Most indicated the original records were generally available at the local church where the sacrament occurred.

Through the years I have benefitted greatly by the Catholic Church's penchant for record keeping. I have also found some intriguing information.

If you're looking for Catholic records in Ireland, there are a number of websites that provide information. Some of the records are online, although most are not. An excellent site is Roman Catholic Records, whose website is *www.irishtimes.com/ancestor/browse/counties/rcmaps/*. A trip to this site provides you with an interactive map of Ireland. All Ireland's counties are displayed, and by clicking on them, you can see what records are available, and whether you can search them yourself, or if you can pay a researcher to review them for you.

Ancestry.com has a rich Catholic records collection. Their collections include:

- Ontario, Canada Catholic Church Records, 1747 — 1967
- Early US French Catholic Church Records, 1695 – 1954
- Brooklyn, NY Catholic Church records, 1837 — 1900
- Brooklyn, NY Catholic Church marriage records, 1839 – 1900

The Catholic Church is a mainstay of genealogists doing research in Europe. While civil registration (government requirements for recording birth, marriage and death information) generally didn't get started until the beginning to middle of the 19th century, the Catholic Church by that time was three hundred years into their record keeping. I spend quite a bit of time detailing Catholic Church records in two *Essentials* books: *Tracing Your European Roots* and *Tracing Your Irish and British Roots.*

With that in mind, here are a few places you can go to locate Catholic records in Europe, England and Ireland:

Ancestry.com has a number of nice collections of parish and civil records from Ireland, including some of the following collections:

- Ireland Births and Baptisms, 1620 -- 1911
- Ireland Catholic parish baptisms, 17 — 42 – 1881
- Irish records extraction database, 1600 -- 1864

Not to be left out, FamilySearch also has more than a few Catholic Church records for Europe:

- France, Coutances Catholic Diocese, 1802 to 1907
- Italy Catania, Arcidiocesi di Catani Civil Registration, 1820 to 1905
- Italy Catania, Arcidiocesi di Catania, Catholic Church records 1515 to 1941
- Aveiro Catholic Church Records
- Portugal baptisms
- Spain baptisms, 1502 to 1940

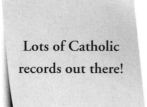

Lots of Catholic records out there!

Jewish Records

As I have worked with Jewish genealogical records, I have been pleased with the amount and accessibility of many Jewish records. Jewish synagogues throughout the world have faithfully kept records of births, deaths and marriages for many generations.

Many of those synagogue records are coming online in recent years. Ancestry.com has a nice collection of Jewish records. To find them, bring up Ancestry.com, then click on *Search*, then click on *Card Catalog*, and type either *Jewish* or *Jewish records*. Immediately you'll be brought to a number of collections that may be of interest to you. Here are a few:

- US, Ohio Cuyahoga County, Jewish Marriage Record Extracts, 1837 – 1934
- US: Hochheimer Marriage Records 1850 — 1900
- Munich, Vienna Barcelona Jewish Displaced Persons and Refugee Cards, 1943 – 1959
- Holocaust: Survivor List from the World Jewish Congress
- Romania: Jewish Names from the Central Zionist Archives

May I vent for a moment? I love Ancestry.com, but sometimes their internal search engine drives me slightly bonkers. Collections I know are there simply cannot be found…unless I go to Google, and type a search string along with the phrase *Ancestry.com*. Let me give you an example: I can go to Google and type *Jewish genealogy*, and one of the first hits I receive is the website *www.ancestry.com/jewishfamily history*. I click on that link and am whisked to a very interesting set of Jewish records held at Ancestry.com. The name of the collection is *Jewish Family History*. However, do you think I could use any combination of words and phrases to bring up these same collections from *within* Ancestry.com? Nope – not going to happen.

So – the lesson of this rant is that if you are not finding the records you want, or even if you do get into some good Jewish records, step back and try Googling various phrases about Jewish genealogy research (along with the phrase *Ancestry.com*) and see what it yields. (And thank you for letting me take a moment to vent.)

Some synagogues kept fastidious track of events such as births, circumcisions, marriages, deaths and burials, and some did not. As I explore Jewish records, it seems to be a mixed bag. According to the Center for Jewish History (*www.cjh.org/p/pdfs/USSynagogueRecords.pdf*), if you are searching for such synagogue records, you should do the following:

1. Locate the synagogue where your ancestors worshipped. This may be accomplished through information contained on documents: wedding, bar-mitzvah and bat-mitzvah invitations, receipts, etc. Or – older relatives may know the synagogue their ancestors attended.
2. If you know the name of the rabbi, but not the synagogue name, there are documents available through the Rabbinical Council of America that can help identify the synagogue where the rabbi served.
3. If the synagogue still exists, contact them and let them know the records

for which you are searching. It would be helpful to be able to share the basics: name(s), approximate birth / circumcision / marriage / death dates, etc.

4. If the synagogue doesn't exist, there are several repositories of synagogue records, including the Center for Jewish History (*www.cjh.org*, 15 West 16th Street, New York, NY. Tel. 212/294-8301).

Speaking of the Center for Jewish History, let's explore that source to see what records they may have available to researchers. Head to their website (*www.cjh.org*), and in the top-middle of the page you'll see a *Search the Collections* section, which contains a *Search* box. In the *Search* box, type: *Synagogue Records* and click on the magnifying glass icon. When I did this, I found 166 hits for my request, including:

• Briesen Community Council Records, 1871 – 1926
• Ostrowo Jewish Community Council 1824 -- 1919 (Births, Marriages, Deaths)
• Musmeah Yeshua Synagogue: Death Register Book, Rangoon Death Register Book, Death Register Book: Musmeah Yeshua Synagogue. 1888 – 1979
• Beth Hamedrash Hagodol 1878 -- 1949

Each of the entries tells you where the records are located, their physical description (book, microfilm, online), the years of the collection, the subject, language the records are written in, and how to arrange to see them. In addition to synagogue records, there are a bevy of records that will assist you in researching your Jewish ancestors. Some of these sources are:

Holocaust Records – many records were kept of the victims and survivors of the Holocaust. In a boon to genealogists researching Jewish roots, as well as Jews themselves, Ancestry.com and the US Holocaust Memorial Museum entered into a partnership to put their holocaust records online, making them accessible to all. You'll find a variety of collections, including Jewish orphans, Czechoslovakian Jews transported to the Terezin concentration camp and other camps, as well as French Jews who were murdered by the Nazis. Over 170 million documents containing the names of approximately 17 million Jews targeted by the Nazis have been put online for researchers to peruse and study. The collections are included in the World Memory Project and are found at *www.worldmemoryproject.org*. The website itself is visually stimulating and user-friendly.

Mohel books – Mohels are the men who performed circumcisions of male children on their eighth day of life. Generally speaking, synagogues did not record births, but Mohel books were kept by synagogues – records of those circumcisions that took place. A typical Mohel book contained required blessings and prayers to be used during the circumcision ceremony, followed by blank pages for the Mohel to record the information about the event. In recent years, Mohel books have been coming online with great frequency. Google *Mohel Books* and you'll get many hits (over 150,000 as of this writing). A good example of what to expect can be found at *www.kehilalinks.jewishgen.org/Lackenbach/html/Mohelbook_Neufeld.html*. Another is *The Mohel Book of Huerben/Krumbach 1800 – 1837 (jgbs.org/ Eruv/Documents/H_Mohelbook.pdf)*. Information included in Mohel books include the date of the event, the child's name and the father's name. Some Mohel books include the name of the town in which the child was born, and some do not. The Center for Jewish History (*www.cjh.org*) also has a collection of Mohel books, searchable by place.

Shtetl Finders – Shtetls are Jewish towns or communities, mostly found in eastern Europe. Shtetl Finders help identify these communities, many of which have ceased to exist. Identifying the shtetl in which your ancestor lived may lead you to other genealogically significant documents and records, such as censuses, Mohel books, synagogue birth, marriage and death records, etc. One of the best websites for assisting in finding a Shtetl is JewishGen on their *KehilaLinks* page (*kehilalinks.jewishgen.org*). Clicking on a geographic region (*The Americas, Asia & Africa, Belarus & Russia*, etc.) takes you to a listing of website links to the Shtetls in that area.

Yizkor Books – these books are labors of love manifested toward victims of the Holocaust, often published by survivors of the same camps where their friends and family members lost their lives. Often, the books are written in Yiddish or Hebrew, and if you're not Yiddish- or Hebrew-literate, translations are available. Yizkor books often include community histories, and include the memories of the survivors about their families, and about many of the individuals who had no family members survive. Generally, a listing of victims is included, along with the names and addresses of those who survived. JewishGen has a wonderful page for Yizkor books (*www.jewishgen.org/Yizkor*) – check it out. They have a significant collection of Yizkor books, many of which have been translated and are available on their website. The *Martyr's List* (also called *The Megillah of the Destruction, Memorial Pages*, etc.) you'll find near the end of many of the Yizkor books is sobering as you scroll through page after page of victims.

One of the best resources I have found for doing Jewish research is JewishGen (*www.jewishgen.org*). What a great website! It is a well-developed website dedicated to Jewish genealogy. It provides advice, counsel and direction. It defines terms for you, answers frequently asked questions, and is the portal to other links and databases that will assist you immensely in your search. Here are some of the highlights of this website:

Jewishgen Discussion Group – this is an e-mail facilitated discussion group that encourages Jewish researchers to share the information they have, methods that have been successful for them in their research, case studies and ideas.

Jewishgen Special Interest Group mailing lists – similar to the Discussion Group, this area focuses on specific areas (geographical or topical) and allows researchers to share the information they have, or to ask questions of those who have researched these specific areas. While not a complete list, at the time of this writing it included places like Belarus, Bohemia-Moravia, Denmark, Germany, Hungary, Latin America, Latvia and Romania. It also included topics such as Rabbinic ancestry, Yizkor books, Stetls (Jewish communities), genetic genealogy, etc.

The Jewishgen Family Finder – a database of over 300,000 Jewish surnames. It is a database of ancestral towns and surnames currently being researched by Jewish genealogists worldwide. Researchers can search records submitted by others as well as submit your own surnames and towns.

As you can see, JewishGen is a website of immense capability and possibilities for those searching their Jewish roots.

Another outstanding website that serves as a superb resource for Jewish genealogical research is The **Federation of East European Family History Societies** (FEEFHS) (*www.feefhs.org*). The FEEFHS consists of a group of dedicated individuals bent on researching, recording and sharing the lives of the people of eastern Europe. Their efforts of course include many of Jewish ancestry.

If your ancestors are Jews who lived in the United Kingdom, you might visit the *Synagogue Scribes* website (*www.synagoguescribes.com/blog*). They contain the records of synagogues, including births, circumcisions, marriages, deaths and burials from throughout the United Kingdom.

Another website with extensive information about Jewish research is that of the **LDS Church**. The LDS Church has an extensive Jewish collection, all of which is available to researchers through the Family History Library in Salt Lake City, or the local Family History Centers, branches of the Family History Library. To learn what sources are available, go to *www.familysearch.org*. From the home page, click on *Research Helps,* then click on *Learn,* then click on either *Research Wiki* or *Research Courses.* I entered *Jewish Research* in the Research Wiki search box, and found over 500 articles on doing Jewish research, including *Jewish Search Strategies, Jewish Archives and Libraries, Jewish Holocaust Records*, and a host of geography-specific Jewish articles (*Jewish Research in Italy, Jewish Research in Poland*, etc.). I back-tracked to Research Courses, and found nearly 150 short video lessons on Jewish research, ranging from 5 minutes to 72 minutes (most were in the 25- to 40-minute range). These articles and videos are full of helpful hints and tips on how to begin and further your search for your Jewish ancestors.

As mentioned throughout this book, the LDS Church's research facilities and records are available to all people interested in genealogy, regardless of religion.

LDS Church Records

Many members of the Church of Jesus Christ of Latter-day Saints (also called Mormons or LDS) are avid genealogists, tracing their ancestors back many generations. The LDS Church is one of the juggernauts in the world of genealogy when it comes to gleaning vital statistics information (birth, marriage and death records) from all over the world. The records they copy from all over the world are made available to all, regardless of religion. Notwithstanding their genealogical activity, they are not particularly strong in sharing the birth, marriage and death information of their own members. Not as a Church entity, anyway. Members of the LDS Church are strongly encouraged to seek out their ancestors. As part of that process, they are encouraged to provide their own vital statistics information to the Church on family group sheets. These family group sheets are included in the Church's mega-database, the International Genealogical Index. It is from this index, among many others, that FamilySearch.org searches when records requests are processed.

However, there are a few collections of records available about members of the LDS Church. If your ancestors were members of the LDS Church, or may have been (if they lived where there were large concentrations of Latter-day Saints, for example), then you'll want to check out some of these sources:

- **Best LDS Websites** – this website is a directory of websites that provide information about LDS Church members. It is located at *www.easyfamilyhistory.com/lds-center/best-lds-websites*. Some collections they point you to include:
- Nauvoo period baptisms – this website lists information about individuals who were baptized for the dead during the Nauvoo period. The website is *www.familyhistory.byu.edu/publications/baptisms.html*.
- *Minnie Margetts File* – this unique file is a listing of members from early English records (1839 – 1913). The index of names is on microfilm, and can be ordered through your local Family History Center. The website for this file is *user.xmission.com/~nelsonb/Minnie*. If you believe you may have had some English ancestors who joined the Mormon Church during that time period, this is definitely worth checking out. Ms. Margetts' file includes a surname index with additional information such as:
  Name of the individual
  Date of birth
  Place of birth
  Parents' names
  Date of baptism, and by whom

Priesthood ordinations

Emigration information

Note: Mormons do not baptize infants. The earliest age Mormons are baptized is at the age of eight years old. These records include the baptismal information of many children over the age of 8 and adults, converts to the Mormon Church during this time period.

- **Early Latter-day Saints** – this website (*www.earlylds.com*), found at *www.earlylds.com*, is a pretty good resource for information on Latter-day Saints who lived between 1830 and 1868. There are a number of records here, including birth, marriage and death records, family histories, pedigree charts and descendant reports. It's pretty interesting to poke around on and see what you can find. It contains the names and information on over 61,000 early members of the Mormon Church.
- **World Vital Records** – (*www.worldvitalrecords.com*) this subscription website has several LDS Collections, including a database containing over 100,000 birth, death and marriage records of Latter-day Saints between 1830 and 1848. Most in the database were residents of Canada, Britain or the United States. You can either purchase a subscription to view this database, or stop by your local Family History Center, which has a library subscription of World Vital Records, and view it there for free.

Lutheran Church Records

Lutherans, like many other churches, kept birth, death and marriage records. One of the quickest ways to locate Lutheran records is to use Google. If you know the congregation or Synod where your ancestors lived, that is best, as you can Google that specifically. Here are a few sites I located in just a few minutes' of Googling:

Concordia Historical Institute – (*www.lutheranhistory.org*) this is a great website that excited me when I read their short historical statement:

> *The Department of Archives and History of the Lutheran Church — Missouri Synod.* From its beginning in 1847, the Synod has provided for its archives, first entrusting the responsibility for maintaining the church's records to the synodical secretary. In 1927 the Institute was incorporated by interested individuals in the church to provide for the preservation of its records. In 1959 the Synod designated the Institute as its official repository.

As well as a short blurb about their collections:

> Concordia Historical Institute has been called "the Library of Congress and the Smithsonian Institute of the Lutheran Church— Missouri Synod." Included in CHI's climate-controlled collection are more than 2.6 million manuscripts, documents, letters, and papers from significant individuals and official church agencies. While Concordia Historical Institute is the Department of History and Archives for The Lutheran Church—Missouri Synod, it also has accumulated a vast collection on the history of Lutheranism in America.

Further research on the website indicated these church records were primarily for the Missouri Synod, which was established in April 1847. There were fourteen original congregations, including congregations in Missouri, Ohio, Illinois and Indiana. There was even one New York congregation (Buffalo / Tonawanda) that was part of the Missouri Synod. From the main page, click on the *Holdings & Collections* tab near the top of the page. Following that, go to *Archives and Manuscripts*. That takes you to a database search page. You can try various ways of searching the databases using assorted search terms. For example, I typed *marriage*, and got 18 hits. Some of the documents contained marriage information, but also contained birth, baptism, confirmation, marriage and death information.

When I typed *death*, I got 33 hits (some of which were included in the hits I received when I searched for marriages).

Each of the entries identified included a description of the items (files, class notes, correspondence, records, family history, lists, etc.), their size (for example: one 3" book, one 200-page book, etc.), and a little history of the item(s) included in the collection.

Records can be researched at the St. Louis location of the Concordia Historical Institute. If you can't make the trek there, they will research records for you for $15 for the first hour, and $30 for each additional hour (free for the first hour and $20 for each additional hour for Institute members). A nice option is inter-library loan, which can be accomplished for $20 per item.

Sometimes, patience is required to search church records.

Evangelical Lutheran Church in America Archives. Another great site for Lutheran church records is the website for the Evangelical Lutheran Church in America (ELCA). Their website is at *www.elca.org*, while information about their genealogy and microfilm collection can be found at *www.elca.org/Who-We-Are/History/ELCA-Archives/Genealogy-and-Microfilm.aspx.* Their web page explains the types of records they have, and indicates that most of the information you are seeking will probably be located in congregational records. If you know your ancestor was Lutheran, you are a step ahead. If you know the congregation he or she was in, that's even better! If not, the ELCA archives folks can help you figure those things out any number of ways. But, as is often the case when you are working with historical documents, the more you know going in, the easier the search is going to be. You may contact the archives at 321 Bonnie Lane, Elk Grove Village, IL 60007, Tel. 847/690-9410, *archives@elca.org*. The archives are open Monday through Friday from 8:30am to 5:00pm.

Microfilmed records are available for rental for $15 per month through inter-library loan processes. Or, if you happen to be in the Elk Grove Village area of Illinois, you may be able to view the records in person. They suggest calling ahead and making an appointment with a reference archivist before you arrive.

If you would like ELCA archivists to research their records for you, they will do that for $20 per hour.

According to their website, the ELCA archives contain the collective memory of the ELCA church-wide organization.

Presbyterian Church Records

Like so many other churches, the Presbyterian Church did not keep centralized records of baptisms, births, marriages or deaths of their members. Rather, what information is available along those lines was typically kept by each individual congregation. So it is important to know – or learn – which congregation your ancestor may have attended.

Often, hints about an individual's congregation can be determined by censuses, naturalization records, state tax records and street directories. Through those records you may be able to determine your ancestor's address or area of town (or township, county, etc.) which may in turn provide a hint as to which Presbyterian congregation your ancestor belonged. You may also have a birth certificate, marriage license or certificate or death certificate signed by a Presbyterian minister – that's a good thing, and will help you identify the specific church to which your Presbyterian ancestor belonged. If you have an address or name of a minister, you can go to *Hall's Index of American Presbyterian Congregations*, which is online at *history.pcusa.org/ collections/hiapc.cfm*. From there you may be able to identify the congregation your ancestor attended, or at least narrow your search to one or two congregations.

Once you have identified a potential Presbyterian church, you can then with some confidence search through church records.

Some records may be kept within the congregation itself. A call to the minister of that congregation is an easy way to ascertain that. Other records may have been centralized to an archival facility. One such location is the *Presbyterian Historical Society* (PHS). Its website is *history.pcusa.org*. Many Presbyterian congregations have yielded their records to the PHS for archival purposes. Many others have not. There is a page on the PHS website that provides you with links to information sites of a number of Presbyterian churches, with contact names and addresses of individual congregations.

PHS also has a searchable database. The search engine is not as forgiving as others like Google or Yahoo, but if you play around with it, you should be able to locate records that may be of interest to you. You can search by subject (birth, marriage, death, etc.) or by congregation name. If you went to *Hall's Index of American Presbyterian Congregations*, for example, and located the church your ancestor likely attended, then enter the name of that congregation to see if they have any of their minutes.

The PHS is located in Philadelphia, and if that's not in your back yard (figuratively speaking) or in the neighborhood of an upcoming trip, they do participate in inter-library loans for their microfilmed holdings. Also, the PHS website says their microfilmed records are available at *FamilySearch.org*, and as you should know by now, you can order those microfilms for just a few dollars, and they will arrive shortly at a local Family History Center. The microfilms will remain there for six weeks for you to peruse.

You will also be successful in finding Presbyterian Church records online for individual congregations. So if you know the name of your ancestor's Presbyterian church, or find the likely congregation through *Hall's Index of American Presbyterian Congregations*, you can Google that congregation. For example: Googling *Second Presbyterian Church, Philadelphia* took me to an interesting set of church records. It began with an interesting history of the congregation, dating back to 1743. It then listed the minutes and reports that were available to researchers. A number of them date to the 18th century. There is a contact address listed for researchers wishing to view these records.

New York City Genealogy has a website that includes church records at *nycnuts.net/genealogy/church/wpa_presbyterian/index.html*. It has links to online pages of the Book Inventory of the Church Archive in New York City – Presbyterian Church in the United States of America.

Quaker Records

Now, before you dismiss this section because your descendants weren't Quakers (as far as you know), may I suggest you at least pause for a moment. If any of your lines go back to Pennsylvania or any of the surrounding states, your ancestors may well have been Quakers. If you'll recall your 8th-grade US History class, you may recall that Quaker William Penn and his followers settled in Pennsylvania.

One of the finest collections of Quaker records is held by Bowling Green University, in Bowling Green, Ohio. The collection is in the Center for Archival Collections, and consists of microfilms of 266 record books containing nearly 200 years of information that dates from 1760 to 1962. Included in the collection are birth, death, marriage and other records of Quakers. Many of the records include father's and mother's names (including maiden names), dates and locations.

This collection can be viewed at Bowling Green State University, or may be able to be ordered through inter-library loans.

Another intriguing source of Quaker church records is found on the Friends Historical Library website (*www.swarthmore.edu/academics/friends-historical-library/quaker-meeting-records.xml*). Located in Swarthmore, Pennsylvania, a number of Quaker records have found their way to this archival library. The most interesting collection I found, and the one most likely to yield the kind of information sought by genealogists, is their Family & Personal Papers collection. You can find the link on the home page, and can alphabetically peruse their holdings of family histories and papers. Unfortunately, the collection is not available through inter-library loan, so you'll need to arrange for a trip to Swarthmore if you find records that seem interesting to you.

Church Records at FamilySearch.org

In addition to searching for church records by individual church / congregation, I have had tremendous success searching for church records at the LDS Church website FamilySearch.org (*www.familysearch.org*). To find church records, go to FamilySearch's website. Click on the *Catalog* label, select *Subject* in the *Search* box, and in the *For* box, type *Church records*. At the time of this writing, that request yielded over 245,000 hits! Examples included the following:

- Birth, baptism, marriage and death records 1861 – 1872, from St. John the
  Baptist, St. Charles Parishes, Louisiana
- Parish Registers for Caton, 1585 – 1900
      Baptisms, marriages, burials, 1585 – 1719
      Baptisms, burials, 1786 — 1812
      Baptisms, burials, 1719 – 1754
      Marriages, 1754 — 1837
- St. Andrew's Presbyterian Church, Church Street: Heppburn, Marriages
  1911 – 1967
- Kirchenbuchduplikat (Duplicate Church Books), 1819 – 1940
      Saint George Catholic Church, Upper Austria
- Primitive Baptist Association Minute Books, 1855 – 1995, Roaring River,
  St. Clair's Bottom, Senter District
- Minutes of the Newfound Baptist Association

Even for the most prolific and persistent genealogists poring over 245,000 entries of church records on FamilySearch.org can be rather daunting. Fortunately, you don't have to – you can narrow the search by specifying the kinds of church records you are seeking: Baptist Church records, Presbyterian Church records, Catholic Church records, Poland church records, France church records, etc. Here are a number of hits I received for some of those specific record searches:

- Baptist church records, 222 hits (some of these were or Catholic churches
  with the name of John the *Baptist* in their name)
- Presbyterian Church records, 451 hits
- Catholic Church records, 600 hits (if you spell Catholic in other languages
  – Katholische, for example, you'll pick up other hits that won't appear
  with the English spelling of Catholic)
- Poland church records, 13,216 hits
- France church records, 38,740 hits

• Italian church records, 2,494 hits

Most of the records you find at FamilySearch.org are on microfilm, but as discussed earlier in this book, those records can be requested by going to a local Family History Center and launching your request. In a week or so, the microfilms you ordered will arrive, and you can view them for up to six weeks at the FHC. Some of the records are beginning to be digitized, and if you run into such records collections, you're in luck – you can open them from your computer and view them to your heart's content. At this point, a small minority of the records held by the LDS Church are digitized, but more are being digitized every day. So – hope for digitization, but settle for microfilms!

> FamilySearch has all kinds of records, including records from many churches.

Church Records at Cyndi's List

Cyndi's List (*www.cyndislist.com*) has a nice collection of church record genealogy sites. If you're not familiar with Cyndi's List, as a genealogist, you should learn to be. It is sort of a large database of websites that cover thousands of areas of genealogy. There is no genealogical content on Cyndi's List, but lots of sites you can go to in order to find genealogical content.

When you reach the home page of Cyndi's List, in the *Search* box at the top of the page, type *Church records*, and you'll be taken to a great cadre of websites that hold great promise for finding church records. As of this writing, Cyndi's List contained nearly 3,000 links to websites for church records. Some were country-specific, others were state specific, and still others were religion specific. Some of them have been included in this book (Ancestry.com, FamilySearch.com, etc.).

One link, entitled *Cyndi's List – Death Records – Locality Specific – Miscellaneous*, took me to over 200 links that included church death records from Mexico, the Czech Republic and Slovakia, Hungary, Yizkor books, Lithuania, Poland, Paris, etc., etc. Often, those links contained links that took me to other links, and so on.

Here's a further peek into Cyndi's list of church records:

• Baptist records – 339 websites
• Catholic records – 1,010 websites
• Jewish records – 1,720 websites
• LDS records – 1,020 websites
• Lutheran records – 198 websites
• Presbyterian records – 184 websites
• Quaker records – 366 websites

So if you run out of places to look for church records, then head on over to Cyndi's List and try your hand with some of her websites.

If your ancestors' churches aren't listed above – never fear. Through these last few pages you've learned some tactics for ferreting out church records. So use the Internet, Ancestry.com, Cyndi's List, FamilySearch, etc. to locate church records for the church and congregation your ancestors attended.

6. BEST GENEALOGY WEBSITES

The Internet is a vast library in the sky where you can find about anything. It is also a great boon to genealogists, and learning to use its power will only help you as you seek to find information about your ancestors through family, library and church records. While there are many genealogy websites out there, following are the ones I have found most helpful for ancestral searches.

Essential Genealogy – *www.essentialgenealogy.com*. This is my website / blog, so I had to give it first place among these other genealogical power-houses. Seriously, it is a place where you can find a genealogy blog, where I share information about research, new and significant sets of genealogy records that have come out, research tactics and tools. There is a section with helpful forms which are free to download: family group sheet, pedigree chart, research log, and templates for:

- Census templates for all the US censuses
- World War I draft registration cards (three templates)
- World War II draft registration cards (old men's draft)
- Day of the week calendars (these help you determine the day of the week a particular date was)

Other features of my website include links to some of my favorite genealogy websites, occasional contests, and giveaways. We're even planning to offer genealogical research services.

Ancestry.com – *www.ancestry.com.* One of two 800-pound gorillas on the genealogy website landscape, Ancestry.com is a tremendous asset for genealogists. For years I resisted paying the subscription fees for Ancestry, eschewing them for free sites. But eventually I had a change of heart, and am glad I

> Check out Dan's favorite websites – free things there!

did. Their collections are varied and impressive, and have been especially helpful in finding church records. And since its rather expensive to travel the world, their international subscription has allowed me to carry on genealogical research in far-away lands from the comfort of my home office.

FamilySearch.org – *www.familysearch.org.* FamilySearch is the other 800-pound gorilla you'll run into constantly while you are searching for church records or other information about your ancestors. Their collections rival those held by Ancestry.com. To be honest, even though FamilySearch is a sentimental favorite, I think Ancestry.com's collections are easier to locate (but even they aren't the best out there!). Unlike Ancestry.com, FamilySearch is free to genealogists. The primary difference between the two (other than free vs. subscription services) is that most of FamilySearch's collections are contained on microfilms. The microfilms can be viewed in the LDS Church's Family History Library in Salt Lake City, Utah, or ordered for a nominal fee and sent to any of over 4,500 Family History Centers around the world.

One of the great aspects of FamilySearch is the learning opportunities they provide, through 67,000+ articles and many videos. For example: your ancestors are from Nova Scotia and you have no clue on where to begin doing genealogical research there? FamilySearch has 150 articles on how to do research in Nova Scotia. They also have a number of video courses ranging between five minutes and 60 minutes on how to do research in Nova Scotia.

Daughters of the American Revolution Genealogical Society – *www.dar.org*. The DAR is a marvelous genealogy society that has been doing it – and doing it right – since 1890. The "it" in this instance, is preserving genealogical records. They have chapters all over the United States and a plethora of genealogy records just waiting to be explored.

National Archives (NARA) – *www.archives.gov*. This government website provides you access to the nation's records – censuses, military, immigration, naturalization, etc. A vast storehouse of information, copies of records can be ordered, viewed in Washington DC or possibly in one of fourteen regional National Archive facilities. Many of the records currently held by NARA are finding their way online through the efforts of NARA as well as subscription services like Ancestry.com and Fold3. For those records not online (most of their records) you can find them on microfilm. But recent years have seen an escalation in the number of online records NARA is providing. This is a fine website to just poke around on, just following your nose to this record set or that image.

Random Acts of Genealogical Kindness — *www.raogk.org*. In late 2011, one of the founders of this fine website, Bridgett Schneider, passed away, and as of this writing, the group isn't back up yet. In the meantime, check them out on Facebook: *www.facebook.com/groups/33868082803/*.

But you should bookmark the website listed above for RAOGK and check it frequently for when it comes back. It represents all that is great about genealogy – genealogists helping genealogists. As a volunteer, you let the RAOGK staff know the acts of genealogical kindness you are able and willing to perform. The administrator then matches you with requests from other genealogists. For example, I volunteered for awhile with RAOGK. I worked several blocks from the Colorado State Library and the Colorado State Archives location in Denver, Colorado. The RAOGK staff would send me requests from genealogists from all over the world – my furthest request was from someone in Australia. The requests were typically for things like obituaries in local newspapers, divorce decrees, birth announcements in papers, etc.

The Facebook page above that is taking the place of RAOGK at the time of this writing, is functioning more or less like a message board. The day I wrote this, the following request was posted:

> I hope there is someone who can find an obit and cemetery for my husband's great grandfather. Erick Ersson Lund B. 30 Aug 1857 in Sweden. Died 11 Aug 1929 Los Angeles, Ca. Thank you for your help as this has become a wall that we can't seem to get over.

Within 24 hours, a photograph of an obituary was posted that read:

> **LUND.** At 1749 West Twenty-Third Street, August 11, Erick Lund. Aged 72 years and husband of Ella and father of Fred A., Leon R., Henry W. Lund and Mrs. E. H. Roe.
> Funeral services at Breese Brothers chapel, 855 Figeroa, 2:00pm Tuesday.

Let's hope RAOGK comes back up firing on all cylinders soon – it was a wonderful program.

Cyndi's List – *www.cyndislist.com*. When you think of Cyndi's List, think of a mammoth card catalog in the sky — it is a gigantic index of genealogical websites. When you go to Cyndi's List, one of the first things you see will be the number of active links available through Cyndi's List. It seems that every time I log onto Cyndi's List, the number of websites grows.

In addition to being an index, Cyndi's List provides links to each website listed, so once you find a website that catches your interest, you merely click on the link and you are there. It is remarkably user friendly, and provides a great service for genealogists. If there is a weakness on Cyndi's List, it is the many, many website links that are there. You'll be like a kid in a candy store, bedazzled and unsure where to turn next.

Message boards – Message boards are fostered by numerous subscription services (Ancestry, Rootsweb, etc.) but the message boards are free. These are great places to seek and find information about ancestors, and find people who are connected with you through your and their genealogical research.

7. A GENEALOGIST'S LIBRARY

As you are aware, there are many, many books written about genealogical research. Below are the books I think need to be in every genealogist's home library. Some are somewhat pricey (like *The Source*), so you may have to wait awhile to pick them up. Or – as long as you know what they are the information they provide, you may decide to use the pricier ones in the genealogy section at your local library.

1. *Secrets of Tracing Your Ancestors,* W. Daniel Quillen. Okay, so this may be a little self-serving, but seriously, in addition to being a genealogy guide for beginners, you will find some advanced tidbits in this book that will help you overcome some of those stumbling blocks you have come across in your research. It includes in-depth research techniques, for example, for numerous areas of ethnic research, including African American, Native American, Jewish, Hispanic, German and Irish research. Here's what one reviewer said about *Secrets of Tracing Your Ancestors*:

> "Shows those new to the hobby how to begin, while showing seasoned family historians some new tricks … with passion and a touch of humor." – *Family Chronicle Magazine*

2. *The Troubleshooter's Guide to Do-It-Yourself Genealogy,* W. Daniel Quillen. *Troubleshooter's* picks up where I left off in *Secrets of Tracing Your Ancestors.* It focuses on research strategies and tactics that assist more

experienced researchers as well as those of any skill level who have run into formidable brick walls in their genealogical research.

3. *Quillen's Essentials of Genealogy series,* W. Daniel Quillen (various titles and editions.). From the opening chapters of this book, you learned a little more about the *Essentials* series of genealogy books. Like this book (*Mastering Family, Library and Church Records*), the books in the *Essentials* series provide a more focused dive into various aspects of genealogical records. To date, the series consists of six titles, including this one:

• *Mastering Online Genealogy*
• *Mastering Immigration & Naturalization Records*
• *Mastering Census & Military Records*
• *Tracing Your European Roots*
• *Tracing Your Irish & British Roots*
• *Mastering Family, Library & Church Records*

Some of these books are already in their second editions and have had multiple printings. Now that the shameless self-promotion is over, let's see what other books need to be in your personal genealogy library:

4. *The Source – A Guidebook to American Genealogy*, Loretto Dennis Szucs and Sandra Hargreaves Luebking (editors), third edition, (Ancestry Publishing, 2006). When I think of this book, I think of the word *Encyclopedic*. It is a wonderful resource for genealogists, and covers most of the critical research areas in US genealogy, including censuses, tax and voting records, land records, immigration and naturalization, court house research, church records, newspapers, vital records, probate, and many other topics.

I have yet to come up empty-handed on a topic that I went to *The Source* to discover answers. It provides volumes of information on a score of topics.

5. *How to Do Everything with Your Genealogy*, George Morgan, (McGraw Hill, March 2004). This great book covers a number of genealogical research topics from beginning through relatively advanced research. Various research strategies are discussed, and you'll be able to determine what may be the best strategy for that particularly difficult and elusive ancestor that stays just out of your reach.

Mr. Morgan takes you beyond the shores of the US, directing you to research sources in the UK, Canada and even Australia.

6. *They Came in Ships: A Guide to Finding Your Immigrant Ancestors' Arrival Record*, John A. Coletta, (Ancestry.com, October 1989). This is an excellent source if you have gotten to the shores of the US and need to learn more about those immigrant ancestors of yours. Mr. Coletta helps you understand the immigration processes, and provides in-depth information on how to locate those valuable passenger lists that often contain so much genealogical information. Several chapters focus specifically on how to gain access to sometimes hard-to-find passenger lists. Ports of arrival are also covered in some depth.

7. *They Became Americans: Finding Naturalization Records and Ethnic Origins*, Loretto Dennis Szucs, (Ancestry.com, July 1, 1998). Ms. Szucs lands her second book on my list of top books for genealogists with this book about finding naturalization records. She describes the naturalization process, and points you to those places you will most likely find immigration and naturalization papers. She also discusses what your options are if the records do not appear to exist.

8. *Courthouse Research for Family Historians: Your Guide to Genealogical Treasures*, Christine Rose, (CR Publications, April 2004). Ms. Rose has performed a great service to all of us who will one day need to visit

courthouses to unearth the records of one or more of our ancestors. This book is an excellent source for learning more about the treasures that are locked behind courthouse doors, and how to gain access to those records. Ms. Rose takes you a few steps further by discussing the available records and the best way to use them to maximize their genealogical value.

The author provides several valuable pointers about how to prepare for a visit to a courthouse, then discusses how to work with clerks to gain access to those documents you wish to see.

9. *Family Chronicle Magazine, www.familychronicle.com.* Okay – so this isn't really a book, but it is a valuable resource for anyone who is working on genealogy. $25 a year gets you a great resource, delivered to your door every other month. I have found the articles to be top shelf in their quality, and each edition that comes has fresh new information that is well worth your time as a genealogist. Back issues are available on CD for $15 per year (each CD contains six issues).

Family Chronicle magazine is the only genealogy magazine I subscribe to. 10. I suggest you get a **good atlas** of the United States (or the country you are researching). As you are researching a family and they disappear from the records in which you expect to find them, it is helpful to look at a map and see what other counties / town / or states they may have gone to. Many of my Quillen ancestors lived and died in the southwest corner of Virginia. However, looking at a map of that area tells me they all lived very close to the state boundaries of four states – Virginia, Kentucky, North Carolina and Tennessee. When I couldn't find records in one state, I would just slip over the line into one of these other nearby states and was often rewarded for my knowledge of geography.

11. A **good gazetteer** (place / name dictionary) for the area you are doing your research and covering the timeframe for which you are doing research is a must. For years I had a hard time locating Denver, Oklahoma. Then perusing a gazetteer from the time period of my

> A good gazetteer will save a lot of headaches!

grandmother's birth helped me locate it – now at the bottom of Lake Thunderbird near Norman, Oklahoma! Through the years, towns changed names, new counties were formed, and many other geographical anomalies occurred, conspiring to make your search unnecessarily difficult. Did you know Long Valley, New Jersey used to be called Germantown, New Jersey? Or that Cobh, Ireland used to be called Queenstown? Many of my Quillen ancestors hail from Scott County, Virginia. However, if I search for vital records for Scott County in the 1700s, I won't find any, because Scott County was formed in 1814 by taking parts of Lee, Russell and Washington Counties. And – in 1856, part of Scott County was used to create Wise County. A good gazetteer will help you sort this out.

12. Family histories can be another valuable source of genealogical information for your family. As I mentioned at the outset of this book, genealogy has been a hobby / interest for our forefathers for many generations – extending back to the dawn of our time. As I have scoured various and sundry records through the years, I have been thankful to stumble across family histories that have been written by one distant cousin or another. I own family histories on the Grahams, McColloughs, Quillens / McQuillans, Throckmortons and Sellers lines, all main-line ancestors for me. I am the happy recipient of hard work done by a few individuals, who did their best to identify and document our mutual ancestors. You say you have none of these written for your lines of the family? Don't be so certain. The Internet is a fabulous genealogical tool, and a few minutes spent with Google may yield great results for you in this area.

8. GLOSSARY

Abstract – a term commonly used with wills and deeds, where the critical information in an original document is summarized.

Ancestors – your progenitors, those from whom you descend: parents, grandparents and on up the family tree.

Bulletin Boards – this is a place where individuals can post queries about ancestors. Others read and may (hopefully) respond to these queries, providing important genealogical information. Also called Message Boards.

Census – an enumeration of the population, usually conducted by the government. It may provide only a tabulation of numbers, but often provides the names of everyone living in the household at the time of the census.

Church records – any of a variety of records kept by congregations of a church, including baptism, confirmation, birth, marriage, death and burial information. Sometimes these records are held at the congregation level, and sometimes they are consolidated to one or more archives / libraries.

Compiled Military Service Records – CMSRs were records kept for the Union and Confederate soldiers and officers. Each soldier will have one for each regiment in which he served. Information found in CMSRs includes biographical and medical information, physical description, pay vouchers, marital status and other personal information like leave requests and commendations. CMSRs were not kept for regular Army soldiers and officers.

Database – a software program that contains information that can be searched against various categories. For example, you can query a database looking for all your ancestors who were born in North Carolina, then search the same database for all ancestors named Robert.

Daughters of the American Revolution (DAR) – a well-known genealogical society for those who can prove a connection to an ancestor who fought in the Revolutionary War.

Descendants – those who descend from an individual – their children, grandchildren, etc. Each considers this person their ancestor.

Family Group Sheet -- this is a document that groups a family together under their father. Included will be a man, his wife and all of their children, along with important information about each person, such as their birth, marriage and death dates and places. It is one of the main forms used in genealogy research.

Family History – this term is often used interchangeably with genealogy. It is also used to describe a narrative account of a family, typically going beyond mere statistics and usually including stories and anecdotes of the individual family members.

Family History Centers – local genealogy libraries staffed by volunteers of the LDS Church where genealogists can access the LDS Church's vast genealogical records. They are open to any genealogist, regardless of religious affiliation. Over 4,500 Family History Centers exist around the world.

Family History Library – a large genealogical research library owned and operated by the LDS Church. Staffed by volunteers, it has an enormous amount of worldwide genealogical information that is available to anyone, regardless of religious affiliation.

Family reunion – a gathering of people to whom you are related and whom you don't see very often, who are generally odder than your immediate family, or so it seems. Typically a lot of bragging and general good humor is shared. Sometimes genealogical information is shared during these conclaves.

Gazetteer – a dictionary for places, which gives you information about places (state, county, country, etc.).

Genealogy – the number one hobby in the world. It is a fascinating, scintillating hobby that involves the search for one's ancestors.

Genealogy societies – groups of like-minded individuals who band together to do genealogical research. Societies may focus on geographic area, ethnic research, surname research, etc. Generally consist of people who are obsessed (in a good way) with finding their roots, and assisting others to do the same.

Immigration records – any of various government records produced at the time an individual immigrated to or emigrated from a location. Included are ships passenger lists, oaths of allegiance, etc. Immigration records are often filled with genealogical information.

LDS Church – acronym for the Church of Jesus Christ of Latter-day Saints. Commonly referred to as Mormons. Genealogical powerhouse whose massive genealogical collection is available to individuals of any (or no) religion.

Message Boards - this is a place where individuals can post queries about ancestors. Others read and may (hopefully) respond to these queries. Also called Bulletin Boards.

Mortality schedules – as part of the 1850 through 1880 censuses, a special schedule was completed that listed the names of all individuals who had died in the year previous to the census. Information on their name, age, sex, illness, duration of illness, etc., was provided. Each of these individuals is tied to a family in the regular census. This is an often-overlooked source of genealogical information.

National Archives – abbreviated as NARA, the National Archives are the repository of all the nation's records – censuses, military, etc. A vast storehouse of information, copies of records can be ordered, viewed in Washington DC or possibly in one of fourteen regional National Archive facilities. Many of the records currently held by NARA are finding their way online through the efforts of NARA as well as subscription services like Ancestry.com and Fold3.

Naturalization records — any of various government records produced at the time an individual immigrates to or emigrates from a location. Included are requests for citizenship (also known as citizenship petitions). Naturalization records are often filled with genealogical information.

Parish – an ecclesiastical or governmental unit where genealogical records were often kept.

Paternal - used to describe which line of the family tree you are referring to. Your paternal grandfather is your father's father.

Pedigree Chart - this is a chart that will show at a glance what your "family tree" looks like, by showing in graphic form who your parents, grandparents, great grandparents, etc., are. A limited amount of genealogical information is included. This is an important genealogical form.

Primary Source - these are genealogy records created at the time of the event. A birth certificate that was completed at the time of a birth would be considered a primary source.

Probate – The judicial procedure that investigates and then declares a will valid after a person dies. In its narrowest definition, probate requires the presence of a will, but common usage often extends to all work settling an estate.

Probate records – Court records representing the final disposal of a person's personal and real property after s/he dies. Probate records are a summary that provides information about the person who has died – their name, birth date, death date, individuals who received property and where they lived.

Queries – from a genealogical perspective, requests for information about a particular person or family. This might be on a message board, in a genealogical publication or via e-mail.

Secondary Source -- genealogy records where information is provided much later than the event. A tombstone or death certificate would be considered a primary source for death information, but a secondary source for birth information, since it is likely that the birth information was provided many years after the person's birth occurred.

Street directories – some street directories provide researchers with another way to locate families in a given place at a given time. They provide important and helpful clues for genealogists.

Vital Records - this term is generally used to refer to genealogical records such as birth, marriage and death information. They are also called Civil Registration or Vital Statistics.

Will – A legal document witnessed by several others that represent an individual's wishes for the disbursement of his/her property after their death. It often contains information about family members.

APPENDIX A:
STATE LIBRARIES & ARCHIVES

Alabama

Alabama Public Library Service, *statelibrary.alabama.gov/Content/Index.aspx*

Alabama Department of Archives and History, *www.archives.state.al.us*

Alaska

Alaska State Archives, *www.library.state.ak.us/*

Alaska State Library, *www.library.state.ak.us*

Arizona

Arizona State Library, *www.lib.az.us*

Arkansas

Arkansas State Library, *www.asl.lib.ar.us/*

California

California State Library, *www.library.ca.gov/*

California State Archives, *www.sos.ca.gov/archives*

Colorado

Colorado State Library, *www.cde.state.co.us/cdelib/*

Colorado State Archives, *www.colorado.gov/dpa/doit/archives*

Connecticut

Connecticut State Library and Archives, *www.cde.state.co.us/cdelib/*

Delaware

Delaware State Library, *www.lib.de.us/*

Delaware Public Archives, *archives.delaware.gov/*

District of Columbia, *os.dc.gov/service/research-and-resources*

Florida

Florida State Library and Archives, *dlis.dos.state.fl.us/*

Georgia

Georgia Department of Archives and History, *www.sos.georgia.gov/AR-CHIVES/*

Hawaii

Hawaii State Library, *www.librarieshawaii.org/*

Hawaii State Archives, *portal.ehawaii.gov*

Idaho

Idaho State Library, *lili.org/*

Idaho State Historical Society, *www. history.idaho.gov*

Illinois

Illinois State Library, *www.cyberdriveillinois.com/departments/library/*

Illinois State Archives, *www.cyberdriveillinois.com/departments/archives/home.html*

Indiana

Indiana State Library and Archives, *www.in.gov/icpr/2358.htm /*

Iowa

Iowa State Library, *www.silo.lib.ia.us/*

State Historical Society of Iowa, *www.iowahistory.org*

Kansas

Kansas State Library, *skyways.lib.ks.us/kansas/*

Kansas State Historical Society, *www.kshs.org*

Kentucky, *www.kdla.ky.gov/*

Louisiana

Louisiana State Library, *www.state.lib.la.us/*

Louisiana State Archives, *www.sec.state.la.us/archives/archives/archives-index.htm*

Maine

Maine State Library, *www.state.me.us/msl*

Maine State Archives, *www.state.me.us/sos/arc/*

Maryland

Maryland State Library, *www.statearchives.us/maryland.htm*

Maryland State Archives, *www.mdarchives.state.md.us*

Massachusetts

Massachusetts State Library, *www.state.ma.us/lib/*

Massachusetts State Archives, *www.sec.state.ma.us/arc/arcidx.htm*

Michigan

Michigan State Library and Archives, *www.michigan.gov/libraryofmichigan/*

Minnesota

Minnesota State Library, *education.state.mn.us/MDE/*

Minnesota State Historical Society, *www.mnhs.org*

Mississippi

Mississippi State Library, *www.mlc.lib.ms.us/*

Mississippi State Archives, *www.mdah.state.ms.us/*

Missouri

Missouri State Library, *www.sos.mo.gov/library/*

Missouri State Archives, *www.sos.mo.gov/archives/*

Montana

Montana State Library, *msl.mt.gov/*

Montana Archives and Libraries, *www.statearchives.us/montana.htm*

Nebraska

Nebraska State Library, *www.nlc.state.ne.us/index.html*

Nebraska State Historical Society, *www.nebraskahistory.org/*

Nevada

Nevada State Library and Archives, *nsla.nevadaculture.org/*

New Hampshire

New Hampshire State Library, *www.nh.gov/nhsl/*

New Hampshire State Archives, *www.state.nh.us/state/index.html*

New Jersey

New Jersey State Library and Archives, *www.njstatelib.org/*

New Mexico

New Mexico State Library, *www.nmstatelibrary.org*

New Mexico State Records Center and Archive, *www.state.nm.us*

New York

New York State Library, *www.nysl.nysed.gov/*

New York State Archives and Records, *www.archives.nysed.gov/aindex.shtml*

North Carolina

North Carolina State Library, *statelibrary.dcr.state.nc.us/*

North Carolina Division of Archives, *www.archives.nysed.gov*

North Dakota

North Dakota State Library, *www.library.nd.gov*

North Dakota State Archives, *www.state.nd.us/hist*

Ohio

Ohio State Library, *www.library.ohio.gov*

Ohio State Archives, *www.statearchives.us/ohio.htm*

Oklahoma

Oklahoma State Library, *www.odl.state.ok.us/index.html*

Oklahoma State Archives, *www.odl.state.ok.us/oar/*

Oregon

Oregon State Library, *cms.oregon.egov.com/OSL/Pages/index.aspx*

Oregon State Archives, *arcweb.sos.state.or.us/banners/contactus.htm*

Pennsylvania

Pennsylvania State Library, *www.portal.state.pa.us/portal/server.pt/community/genealogy_and_local_history/8730*

Pennsylvania State Archives, *www.portal.state.pa.us/portal/ server.pt?open=512&mode=2&objID=1426*

Rhode Island
Rhode Island State Library, *www.olis.state.ri.us/*
Rhode Island State Archives, *www.state.ri.us/archives/*
Rhode Island Historical Society, *www.rihs.org*

South Carolina
South Carolina State Library, *www.statelibrary.sc.gov/*
South Carolina Archives and History Center, *scdah.sc.gov/*

South Dakota
South Dakota State Library, *www.sdstatelibrary.com/*
South Dakota State Historical Society, *www.sdhistory.org/*

Tennessee
Tennessee State Library and Archives, *www.tennessee.gov/tsla/*

Texas
Texas State Library and Archives, *www.tsl.state.tx.us/*

Utah
Utah State Library, *library.utah.gov/*

Utah State Archives, *www.archives.state.ut.us*

Vermont
Vermont State Library, *libraries.vermont.gov/*
Vermont State Archives, *vermont-archives.org/*

Virginia

Virginia State Library and Archives, *www.lva.lib.va.us/*

Washington

Washington State Library, *www.sos.wa.gov/library/ /*
Washington State Archives, *www.secstate.wa.gov/archives/search.aspx*

Washington DC

The Library of Congress, *www.loc.gov/index.html*

West Virginia

West Virginia State Library, *www.librarycommission.wv.gov/Pages/default.aspx*
West Virginia State Archives, *www.wvculture.org/history/wvsamenu.html*

Wisconsin

Wisconsin Division of Libraries, *www.dpi.state.wi.us/dpi/dlcl/index.html*
Wisconsin State Historical Society, *www.wisconsinhistory.org/index.html*

Wyoming

Wyoming State Library, *www-wsl.state.wy.us/*
Wyoming State Archives, *wyoarchives.state.wy.us/*

APPENDIX B:
NATIONAL ARCHIVES LOCATIONS

There are a number of locations of the National Archives geographically dispersed around the United States. Each contains a treasure trove of genealogical information, including all the US Censuses that are available for the public to view. Below are the fourteen main locations, but there are many more now, spread throughout the nation. These include Presidential Libraries, microfilm locations, textual research locations, military records locations, Library of Congress, etc. You can find a complete listing at *www.archives.gov/locations*. Following are their locations:

Alaska
654 West Third Avenue
Anchorage, Alaska 99501-2145
Tel. 907/271-2441
E-mail: *alaska.archives@nara.gov*
Website: *www.archives.gov/pacific-alaska/anchorage/index.html*

California
24000 Avila Road,
1st Floor, East Entrance
Laguna Niguel, California 92677-3497
Tel. 949/360-2641
E-mail: *laguna.archives@nara.gov*
Website: *www.archives.gov/pacific/laguna/index.html*

1000 Commodore Drive
San Bruno, California 94066-2350
Tel. 650/876-9009
E-mail: *sanbruno.archives@nara.gov*
Website: *www.archives.gov/pacific/san-francisco/index.html*

Colorado
Bldg. 48, Denver Federal Center
West 6th Avenue and Kipling Street
Denver, Colorado 80225-0307
Tel. 303/236-0806
E-mail: *denver.archives@nara.gov*
Website: *www.archives.gov/rocky-mountain/index.html*

Georgia
5780 Jonesboro Road
Morrow, Georgia 30260
Tel. 770/968-2100
E-mail: *atlanta.archives@nara.gov*
Website: *www.archives.gov/southeast*

Illinois
7358 South Pulaski Road
Chicago, Illinois 60629-5898
Tel. 773/581-7816
E-mail: *chicago.archives@nara.gov*
Website: *www.archives.gov/great-lakes/contact/directions-il.html*

Massachusetts
Frederick C. Murphy Federal Center
380 Trapelo Road

Waltham, Massachusetts 02452-6399
Tel. 781/647-8104
Tel. 866/406-2379
E-mail: *waltham.center@nara.gov*
Website: *www.archives.gov/northeast/boston/*

10 Conte Drive
Pittsfield, Massachusetts 01201-8230
Tel. 413/445-6885
E-mail: *archives@pittsfield.nara.gov*
Website: *www.archives.gov/northeast/boston/*

Missouri
400 West Pershing road
Kansas City, Missouri 64108
Tel. 816/926-6920
E-mail: *kansascity.archives@nara.gov*
Website: *www.archives.gov/facilities/mo/kansas_city.html*

New York
201 Varick Street
New York, New York 10014-4811
Tel. 212/337-1300
E-mail: *newyork.archives@nara.gov*
Website: *www.archives.gov/northeast/nyc/*

Pennsylvania
900 Market Street
Philadelphia, Pennsylvania 19107-4292
Tel. 215/597-3000

E-mail: *philadelphia.archives@nara.gov*
Website: www.archives.gov/midatlantic/agencies/

14700 Townsend Road
Philadelphia, Pennsylvania 19154
Tel. 215/305-2038
E-mail: *philadelphia.archives@nara.gov*
Website: *www.archives.gov/midatlantic/agencies/*

Texas
1400 John Burgess Drive
Fort Worth, Texas 76140
Tel. 817/551-2051
E-mail: *ftworth.archives@nara.gov*
Website: *www.archives.gov/southwest/index.html*

Washington
6125 Sand Point Way NE
Seattle, Washington 98115-7999
Tel. 206/526-6501
E-mail: *seattle.archives@nara.gov*
Website: *www.archives.gov/pacific-alaska/seattle/index.html*

Washington DC
National Archives Building
700 Pennsylvania Avenue, N.W.
Washington DC 20408
Tel. 866/272-6272
Website: *www.archives.gov/*

INDEX

Genealogical Notes

Genealogical Notes

Genealogical Notes